NEW YORK
City Trails

Moira Butterfield

Hi... we're Amelia and Marco and we've created 19 awesome themed trails for you to follow.

The pushpins on the map on the right mark the trail starting points. Each one is sure to let you in to the city's secrets, and blow your mind with cool facts!

To help you find your way around New York's five boroughs, take a look at the map below. Now, whether you are following a trail from Manhattan to Brooklyn, or from Queens to the Bronx, you'll never get lost.

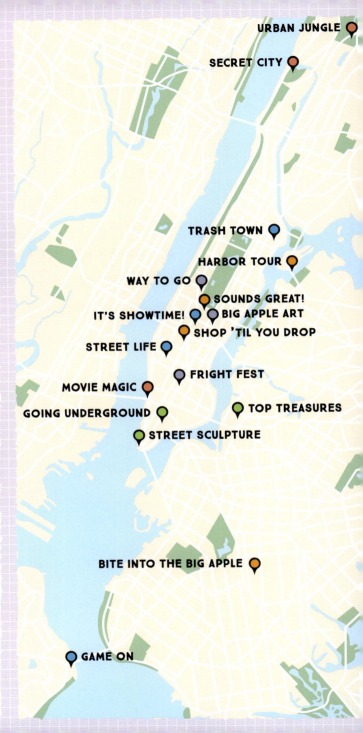

CONTENTS

PAGE NUMBER

- STREET LIFE 6-9
- SKYSCRAPER FLYBY 10-15
- SECRET CITY 16-19
- GREEN NEW YORK 20-25
- TRASH TOWN 26-29
- URBAN JUNGLE 30-35
- GOING UNDERGROUND 36-39
- BITE INTO THE BIG APPLE 40-45
- TOP TREASURES 46-49
- IT'S SHOWTIME! 50-55
- WAY TO GO 56-59
- HARBOR TOUR 60-65
- FRIGHT FEST 66-69
- GAME ON 70-75
- SOUNDS GREAT! 76-79
- BIG APPLE ART 80-85
- STREET SCULPTURE 86-89
- SHOP 'TIL YOU DROP 90-95
- MOVIE MAGIC 96-99

INDEX 100-102

STREET LIFE

With more than 6,000 miles (9,650 km) of roadway, getting hopelessly lost in New York might seem a done deal, but it's surprisingly easy to find your way around the city. Get ready to point your feet along those streets!

BILLION-DOLLAR BELL
WALL STREET

Wall Street is the name given to the whole of the financial district of Manhattan, though it's actually just one street in this megamoneymaking hub. The NYSE (New York Stock Exchange) is the hi-tech heart of Wall Street, where billions of dollars' worth of stocks and bonds are traded daily. It runs on powerful computers, but relies on a simple bell to open and close trading every day. Celebrities vie for the honor of pressing the button that activates the bell.

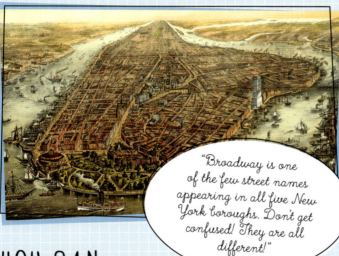

"Broadway is one of the few street names appearing in all five New York boroughs. Don't get confused! They are all different!"

YOU CAN COUNT ON IT
MANHATTAN'S GRID

Who needs GPS when you have Manhattan's great grid system! This amazing master plan for the city's layout dates back to 1811, when the roads were mainly just dirt tracks and needed organizing. The city commissioners chose the grid design because it was a great way to fit more houses in.

THE AVENUES RUN NORTH TO SOUTH, AND THE STREETS RUN EAST TO WEST. THE CORNER OF 1ST STREET AND 1ST AVENUE IS WHERE THE NUMBERS START FROM. THEY GET HIGHER TO THE WEST AND NORTH. EVERYTHING IS THE OPPOSITE IN QUEENS.

> NIKOLA TESLA CORNER

BRILLIANT BIRDMAN
NIKOLA TESLA CORNER

Nikola Tesla was the first person to discover radio waves, and he did much of his work in a hotel near this spot. Although he patented his radio discovery, other inventors benefited from his work and became famous, leaving poor old Nikola to die penniless and obscure. The local pigeons loved him, though. He fed them in Bryant Park, and this corner of town is named after him because it's where he cared for his beloved birds. We salute your street corner, nice Nikola!

CELEBRITY SQUEEZE
75½ BEDFORD STREET

This is New York's narrowest house, found in Greenwich Village. Although it's only 9 feet (2.7 m) wide, it's been home to celebrity movie stars in its time, and it comes with a giant price tag. It was last sold for US$3.25 million to a buyer whose wallet was pretty big, even if his new home was not.

> BEDFORD STREET

PEACE PLACE
UNITED NATIONS HQ

405 East 42nd Street is not even technically part of the US, let alone part of New York. It's the address of the UN (United Nations) headquarters and it's designated as international territory. The flags of all the UN member states are flown outside, in alphabetical order. Inside, the UN has its own fire department, police force, and post office, with its own stamps!

THE UN BUILDING HAS A MAGICAL HIDDEN ROSE GARDEN, WITH ITS OWN PAGODA SYMBOLIZING WORLD PEACE.

UNITED NATIONS HQ

6½ AVENUE

WHEEL-FREE WALK
6½ AVENUE

There's a street in New York with no traffic jams or noisy car alarms. In fact, there aren't any vehicles. Foot-friendly 6½ Avenue is a pedestrian walkway in Manhattan that runs between, and sometimes through, a string of high-rise buildings, parks, and squares from West 57th to West 51st Street. It's around 0.25 miles (0.4 km) of welcome wheel-free walking.

STONE HOME
COLUMBUS CIRCLE

Columbus Circle marks the official center of New York City. It's surrounded by a circle of fountains and has a statue of explorer Christopher Columbus in the middle. In 2012, artist Tatzu Nishi built a living room around Columbus, giving him all his own furniture and even a flat-screen TV. For a while anyone could climb up the stairs to visit the statue's arty apartment.

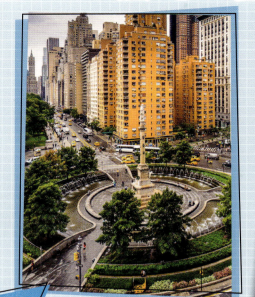

search: CHRISTOPHER COLUMBUS

A NEW WORLD?

Columbus was an explorer. In 1492, he set sail from Spain and crossed the Atlantic in search of new trade routes. When Columbus set out, he was expecting to eventually reach the Far East. Instead, he landed on the shores of America – a continent that was unknown to Europeans at the time.

COLUMBUS CIRCLE

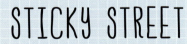

STICKBALL BOULEVARD

STICKY STREET
STICKBALL BOULEVARD, BRONX

Stickball is a game long played by kids without access to baseball equipment or a field. Instead, they improvise with a broom handle, a rubber ball, and anything they can find to use as bases, including manhole covers, fire hydrants, cars, or even someone's little brother! Stickball Boulevard in the Bronx is named after the game, and now there's an official New York Stickball League and an annual tournament. On weekends, a couple of blocks are kept car-free so that stickball teams can play there.

9

SKYSCRAPER FLYBY

This fabulous flight past some of the city's skyscrapers is a salute to Elisha Otis, who has to be one of New York's big heroes. Why? Because he invented the first elevator with brakes in 1852. Without him, New Yorkers would have to take a LOT of stairs.

432 PARK AVE.

QUEENS MUSEUM OF ART

TINYTOWN
QUEENS MUSEUM OF ART

Those without a head for heights can still get a bird's-eye view of NYC at the Queens Museum of Art, where the Empire State Building is only 15 inches (38 cm) tall and the Statue of Liberty is about the size of a thumb. The panorama of the city features mini-models of 895,000 New York buildings, along with 100 bridges and even tiny wire-mounted planes flying in and out of the city's LaGuardia Airport.

START

SKY-HIGH SLEEPING
432 PARK AVE.

Welcome to the highest rooftop in New York, at a height of 1,396 feet (425.5 m). One of the tallest residential buildings in the world, the design of this 96-story tower was inspired by the shape of a trash can. Its luxury apartments are far from trashy, though. The six-bedroom, seven-bathroom penthouse on top was on sale for the superhigh price of US$95 million in 2014.

601 LEXINGTON

ROCKEFELLER CENTER

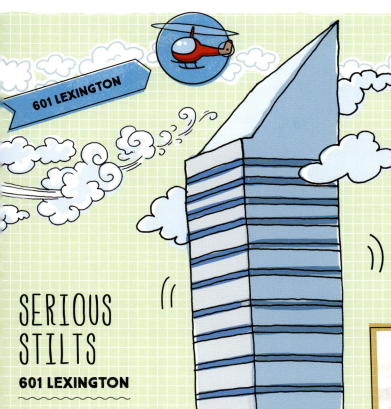

NOW THAT'S HIGH
TOP OF THE ROCK, ROCKEFELLER CENTER

This famous *Lunch Atop a Skyscraper* photo, showing workers eating lunch on a superhigh steel beam, was taken in 1932 during the construction of Rockefeller Center. The building still has one of the best views around, though you can now go inside and up to the 70th floor to get the full New York experience – 850 feet (260 m) above the street!

SERIOUS STILTS
601 LEXINGTON

601 Lexington was built with its bottom nine stories as four massive stilts. It was designed that way to accommodate a church on the site beneath the building. The only problem was that the position of the stilts left the skyscraper dangerously vulnerable to high winds. Once the threat became clear, something had to be done – and fast! As work secretly began to reinforce the building, Hurricane Ella was heading for New York! Luckily, Ella never made landfall, so the tower was saved and is now ultrasafe.

"Don't look down!"

THE FIRST SKYSCRAPERS HAD 10-20 STORIES. TODAY, SKYSCRAPERS NEED 40+ STORIES TO GET THE NAME.

CHRYSLER BUILDING

EMPIRE STATE BUILDING

1,048 FT. (319 M) TALL TO THE TIP

1,454 FT. (443 M) TALL TO THE TIP

WINNING POINT
CHRYSLER BUILDING

By the late 1920s, the battle for the world's tallest building was heating up, and the architects of the Chrysler Building and 40 Wall Street went head-to-head in the battle for the top spot. The height of 40 Wall Street was increased, but the Chrysler Building had a secret weapon — a 124-foot 8-inch (38 m) spire that was being assembled inside the tower. When this was finally hoisted to the top, the Chrysler Building claimed the title.

LIT UP AND LOVELY
EMPIRE STATE BUILDING

Less than a year after the Chrysler Building opened, the Empire State Building stole its crown and went on to hold the title of world's tallest building for over 40 years. The lights that illuminate the top 30 floors at night traditionally change color to celebrate holidays and events, such as Christmas or Valentine's Day. If you ever want an extreme fitness challenge, the ESB hosts an annual race up 1,576 steps to the 86th floor.

12

SKY SLICE
FLATIRON BUILDING

At 22 stories, the wedge-shaped Flatiron was never the city's tallest building, but it soon became a much-loved New York icon. Public opinion wasn't always so positive though. The *New York Tribune* once called it "a stingy piece of pie," while the locals took bets on how far the debris would spread when it blew down. The building proved more than strong enough to withstand the wind, athough downdraughts lifted the skirts of lady shoppers below! The Flatiron measures less than 6.56 feet (2 m) across at the narrow end.

CASH CATHEDRAL
WOOLWORTH BUILDING

The Woolworth Building lost its title as the world's tallest many years ago, but its cathedral-like lobby is still one of the most spectacular. Salamander lizards decorate the interior to represent the tower's fireproof construction (salamanders were once thought to survive fire), and statues of those involved in the building crouch in corners, holding something to show their role: owner Frank Woolworth holds a nickel, architect Cass Gilbert holds a model of the building, and builder Louis Horowitz has his ear to an old-fashioned phone.

307 FT. (93.6 M) TALL

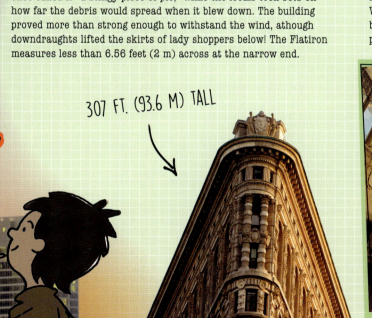

MR. WOOLWORTH PAID US$13.5 MILLION FOR THE BUILDING — IN CASH.

13

FREEDOM TOWER

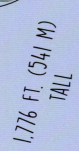

ONE WORLD TRADE CENTER

ONE WORLD TRADE CENTER

One World Trade Center is New York's tallest tower. When the last part of the spire was fitted, the tower reached its final height of 1,776 feet (541 m) – a reference to 1776, the year when the US Declaration of Independence was signed. It's nicknamed "Freedom Tower," and opened in November 2014, 13 years after the World Trade Center's Twin Towers were destroyed.

AROUND AND BELOW

Visitors to the observatory can see below as well as all around. The street beneath their feet can be "seen" through the Sky Portal, which shows real-time video footage from below.

1,776 FT. (541 M) TALL

SUPERFAST RIDE

Seventy-three state-of-the-art elevators carry people up the building. Five of these are express elevators. They whizz from the ground floor to the observatory on the 102nd floor in less than a minute at a top speed of 23 mph (37 km/h).

HIGHEST TOWER IN THE WESTERN HEMISPHERE AND THE FOURTH TALLEST IN THE WORLD

NIGHT HEIGHT

The giant pieces that made up the spire had to be delivered on an extrawide truck in the middle of the night, so as not to cause chaos in the streets of New York.

14

22,500
NUMBER OF CARS THAT COULD BE MADE OUT OF THE STEEL IN THE BUILDING

13,000
GLASS PANELS USED ON OUTSIDE OF BUILDING

search: FREEDOM TOWER

CONCRETE CRAZY
It has been calculated that the Freedom Tower contains enough concrete to lay a thick path from New York to Chicago.

REMEMBERING 9/11
One World Trade Center overlooks the twin pools of the National September 11 Memorial. The pools sit within the footprints of where the Twin Towers once stood, and the names of those who died are carved on bronze panels around their edges. The nearby 9/11 Museum contains images and artifacts from the towers.

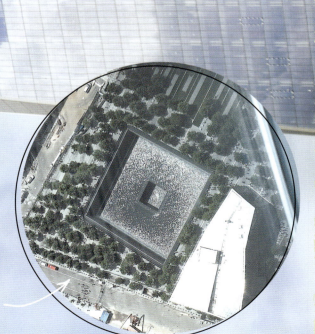

SECRET CITY

Tiptoe along this trail of mysteries to discover New York's secret world of ghostly tunnels, rooftop forests, and bank vaults filled with gold. Here, smugglers once stashed their booty, gangsters made their getaways, and ancient bones lay hidden!

GRAND CENTRAL TERMINAL

CARELESS WHISPERS
WHISPERING GALLERY, GRAND CENTRAL TERMINAL

Whispering secrets is a popular pastime at Grand Central Terminal. There's an area of archways on the way down to the lower concourse where messages can be whispered to the wall and heard by someone listening at the wall diagonally opposite, 33 feet (10 m) away! New Yorkers call it the Whispering Gallery, and it's caused by the stone walls and ceiling reflecting sound across the underpass.

INDIAN CAVES — START

ANCIENT NY CAMPSITE
INDIAN CAVES

For centuries the ancient caves in Inwood Hill Park were used as a campsite by the Lenape tribe, probably because they could go fishing in the river nearby. In the 1640s, the tribe was driven away, but they left behind pottery, tools, and weapons, including polished flint axe heads. These are now safely looked after at the New York branch of the National Museum of the American Indian.

16

OFFICE IN A FOREST
FORD FOUNDATION GREENHOUSE

It's an unlikely place to find a tropical rainforest, but the Ford Foundation, an office building on East 43rd Street, is bursting with giant trees, shrubs, and steamy pools. Made from glass and steel, the building works like a giant greenhouse. Rain is collected on the roof to water the plants and add to the humid atmosphere.

FORD FOUNDATION GREENHOUSE

THE FORD FOUNDATION GREENHOUSE IS 160 FT. (49 M) HIGH!

BLOODY ANGLE

GANGSTER GETAWAY
"BLOODY ANGLE"

Back in the early 1900s, Doyers Street in Chinatown was known as the "Bloody Angle" because its curved shape meant rival gangs could creep up on each other unseen. There were street battles and murders, and a network of tunnels under the road helped the gangsters to escape. Today, the last remaining tunnel is lined with shops, offices, and bars.

STEAM CITY

STEAM TUNNELS

Spooky wisps of steam can sometimes be seen escaping from New York's manhole covers and from striped street pipes, giving the city a haunted look at night. The steam comes from an underground maze of pipes that connect to around 2,000 buildings from generating stations. It's used for heating and cooling buildings, running restaurant dishwashers, and sterilizing hospital equipment. Safety valves and leaks produce the steam wisps.

AROUND MANHATTAN

search: GOLD BARS

📍 PURE GOLD

Gold bars are not made of pure gold, as it is too soft and the bars would not hold their shape. Each bar contains a small amount of another metal, such as iron, silver, or platinum. This makes the bars hard enough to stack and store for long periods of time.

FEDERAL RESERVE BANK

UNDERGROUND GOLD

FEDERAL RESERVE BANK

This is the granddaddy of Manhattan treasures. It's the biggest stash of gold bars in the world, and it's hidden behind thick steel walls in a vault 80 feet (24.3 m) below the street. There are around 530,000 bars in the vault, which has to rest on the solid bedrock beneath Manhattan because the bars are so heavy. The gold belongs to different governments around the globe and is worth billions.

FOR SECURITY, THREE OFFICIALS MUST BE PRESENT EVERY TIME A COMPARTMENT IN THE VAULT IS OPENED — EVEN IF IT'S JUST TO CHANGE A LIGHTBULB!

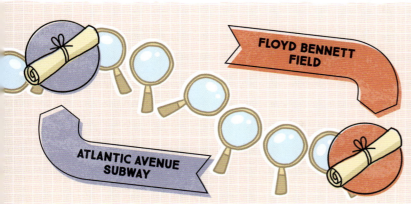

SMUGGLERS' SUBWAY
ATLANTIC AVENUE SUBWAY

Built in 1844, the Atlantic Avenue tunnel is the world's oldest subway tunnel. It was built for early steam trains, which were banned from traveling through town because they had bad brakes and blew up every now and then! The tunnel was closed to trains in the 1860s, but legend has it that smugglers used it to stash stolen goods. There are even rumors that a gangster's body was once hidden down there.

> THE ATLANTIC AVENUE SUBWAY WAS FORGOTTEN AFTER WORLD WAR II, WHEN THE AUTHORITIES SEARCHED IT FOR SPIES. IT WAS NOT REDISCOVERED UNTIL 1981.

PUPPET PIRATE GOLD
FLOYD BENNETT FIELD

In 2009, a team of puppeteers buried a US$10,000 hoard of dollar coins in a secret location. They left clues in a series of videos featuring a pirate puppet and his parrot. People searched the city for nearly three years – but to no avail. Finally, in 2012, the puppeteers dug up the treasure (in woods next to Floyd Bennett Field) and donated it to charity.

GREEN NEW YORK

OK, so New York is one of the world's biggest cities, but that doesn't mean it's all high-rise buildings and busy streets. Here and there, hidden away, there are precious pockets of green space where city-dwellers can chill. So pack your picnic basket and wander this way...

QUEENS COUNTY FARM MUSEUM

DOWN ON THE FARM
QUEENS COUNTY FARM MUSEUM

This amazing farm has been going since 1697, when most of the city we see today was still countryside. It has been planted continuously for more than 300 years, while the teeming town has grown up around it. Pigs, sheep, hens, honeybees, and goats live here, along with some cute Dexter cattle. They're among the world's smallest cattle, growing to only around 40 inches (102 cm) high.

BLOSSOM AND BONSAI
BROOKLYN BOTANIC GARDEN

This beloved green space in Brooklyn is a must-see in springtime, when it turns pink with the blossoms of more than 200 cherry trees. It's a welcome sign that the chilly NY winter is over. The gardén also has one of the world's best collections of bonsai trees, some of them more than 300 years old. The oldest bonsai tree specimens can sell for over US$1 million each, so the tiny trees kept here are one of the city's true treasures!

BROOKLYN BOTANIC GARDEN

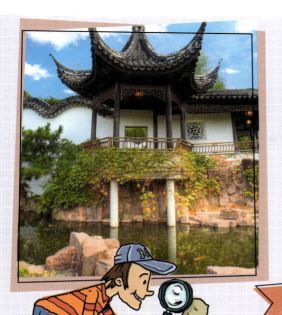

WATCH A ROCK
NY CHINESE SCHOLAR'S GARDEN, SAILORS' SNUG HARBOR

This garden was built by a team of 40 artists and gardeners from China, taking inspiration from the best Chinese gardens in history. The rockery symbolizes the mountains that once inspired Chinese poets and artists. Visitors can also enjoy the "scholar's rocks" — natural rocks with interesting shapes and colors, carefully positioned for people to sit and study.

Some scholar's rocks look like animals, birds, humans, or mythical beasts. Others are admired for their resemblance to caves or mountain peaks.

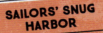

SAILORS' SNUG HARBOR

LIZ CHRISTY COMMUNITY GARDEN

A SEED IS PLANTED
LIZ CHRISTY COMMUNITY GARDEN

In 1973, an environmental group called the Green Guerillas started throwing "seed bombs" (packets full of seeds and fertilizer) over fences into vacant lots on the Lower East Side of Manhattan. Plants soon sprouted, and the idea itself eventually grew into this oasis of plant power, the city's first community garden. Liz Christy was one of the people who helped get it going, and the garden is named in her memory.

FREE FOREST
NEW YORK EARTH ROOM, 141 WOOSTER STREET

In 1977, artist Walter De Maria installed a layer of soil nearly 22 inches (56 cm) deep across the floor of a large apartment in SoHo, to make an earthy art installation. Anyone can visit for free, and those who go say it's a surprisingly calm and peaceful place to be. *The New York Earth Room* looks like a deep carpet. You can't touch it, but you can smell it because the dirt is kept moist, so it gives off the scent of a forest floor. A full-time caretaker rakes and waters the soil – and gets to eat the mushrooms that occasionally sprout!

WOOSTER STREET

GRAMERCY PARK

NO KEY, NO SEE
GRAMERCY PARK

There's one private park left in NYC. It's been going since 1831, and it's only open to residents of nearby buildings who pay for a precious key to the gate. Lots of things are banned, including pets, Frisbees, ball games, bird-feeding, squirrel-feeding, and taking photos. One visitor caused a scandal when he posted photos on Google Maps. The park is open to the public on Christmas Eve... for one hour.

search: NY PARK FACTS

1,700
The city has over 1,700 parks and places to play.

14%
Nearly 14 percent of NYC is covered with green spaces.

PELHAM BAY PARK
NY's biggest park is in the Bronx, covering 4.25 square miles (11.2 sq km) of land.

"NO photos!"

WEST SIDE

PALEY PARK

MINI-MARVELS
PALEY PARK AND OTHER LOCATIONS

Because Manhattan is packed with buildings, many of its parks have to be small. They're called "pocket parks," and Paley is one of people's favorites. It's not bursting with greenery, but it does have a wall of water 20 feet (6.1 m) high that helps to drown out traffic noise. Greenacre Park has an even bigger waterfall that's 25 feet (7.6 m) high, making a splash right in the middle of Midtown.

NATURAL TRACK
HIGH LINE, MANHATTAN'S WEST SIDE
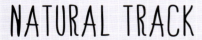

Here's a park that's perfect for a sky stroll. It's been created along an old elevated train track, long after the last train ran in 1980. This is a place to sit and watch the traffic go by below you, or to peek into nearby buildings if you're feeling nosy. Unlike many parks, where the plants are brought in and planted, the park designers here welcome "volunteer" plants that sprout wild on the tracks. Along the route there's art on show, a miniature forest, and even deck chairs and a water feature for track-side toe-paddling.

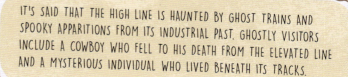
IT'S SAID THAT THE HIGH LINE IS HAUNTED BY GHOST TRAINS AND SPOOKY APPARITIONS FROM ITS INDUSTRIAL PAST. GHOSTLY VISITORS INCLUDE A COWBOY WHO FELL TO HIS DEATH FROM THE ELEVATED LINE AND A MYSTERIOUS INDIVIDUAL WHO LIVED BENEATH ITS TRACKS.

THE BIG ONE

CENTRAL PARK

Central Park covers around 1.3 square miles (3.4 sq km) of Manhattan, and is one of the most famous parks on the planet. It's been a nature haven for New Yorkers for over 150 years. Here are some particularly peculiar park facts that may surprise you!

GOOD FOR GREENERY

Wealthy New Yorkers lobbied to have the park built as a place to ride their carriages, and because they thought it would encourage people out of the town's taverns. The location was chosen because the land there was covered in swamps and rocks and was difficult to build on. A competition was held for the best design.

LOTTA LEGS

As you'd expect, all sorts of wild creatures live in Central Park, including beetles, spiders, bats, and owls – but the big surprise was a brand-new species of centipede discovered here in 2002. Ten of the tiny 82-legged critters were found and, at around 0.4 inches (10.3 mm) long, they turned out to be the smallest centipedes in the world. They were given the name Hoffman's dwarf centipede. It's thought they may have arrived from Asia in a batch of imported plants.

AROUND 37.5 MILLION PEOPLE VISIT THE PARK EVERY YEAR...

25,000 TREES

58 MILES (93 KM) OF PATHWAYS

36 BRIDGES & ARCHES

7 BODIES OF WATER

...MAKING IT THE BUSIEST CITY PARK IN THE US.

STINKY PIG PLACE

The stinky job of boiling animal bones used to take place on the west side of the park, and pig farmers lived in the southeastern corner, in a village known as Pigtown. Sheep grazed in the area called Sheep Meadow until 1934, but were taken away in case hungry people decided to eat them during the Depression (a time when many people lost their jobs and often went without food).

AROUND 1,600 LOCAL PEOPLE HAD TO BE MOVED OFF THE LAND TO BUILD THE PARK.

DARING DOG

There are 29 sculptures in the park, including the likeness of a famous Alaskan doggie hero, Balto. In 1925, for a snowy six days, he led a team of huskies over 990 miles (1,600 km) from the Alaskan city of Anchorage to the town of Nome, carrying a vital serum that prevented people dying in an outbreak of the deadly disease diptheria.

TRASH TOWN

They say one person's trash is another person's treasure. New York certainly produces a lot of trash, and it's true that some of it is recycled in interesting ways. Ride on the garbage truck to discover some of the precious facts we've plucked from the trash cans around town.

TRASH MUSEUM

TREASURE IN TRASH
TRASH MUSEUM, EAST HARLEM

A garage in East Harlem is home to a secret invitation-only museum. It houses a stash of interesting trash found by Nelson Molina during his 28 years as a sanitation worker. He calls it the "Treasures in the Trash Museum," and it's a fantastic snapshot of daily stuff used around the city, from toys and furniture to art and household gadgets. Even the walls are painted with paint found by Molina on his rounds.

SUCCESS SUCKS
PNEUMATIC TRASH TUBES, ROOSEVELT ISLAND

You won't find many garbage trucks in the Roosevelt Island part of town. That's because it has its own hidden garbage-sucking secret called the AVAC – a system of pipes running under all the high-rise buildings. When residents throw their garbage down the chutes, air valves suck it through underground tubes and it shoots at up to 60 mph (96.5 km/h) to the northern corner of the island, where it gets packed into containers. Problems only happen if thoughtless people block the pipes by throwing away extra large trash.

ROOSEVELT ISLAND

RECLAMATION ROOM

GRAND CENTRAL STATION

The Lost and Found department at Grand Central Station is the destination for things that are left behind by train travelers. Tens of thousands of objects arrive here every year and roughly half are reunited with their owners. Cell phones are the most common lost items, but there have been all kinds of strange things left behind, including prosthetic limbs, a violin worth US$100,000, baseball tickets, and a singing President Bush doll.

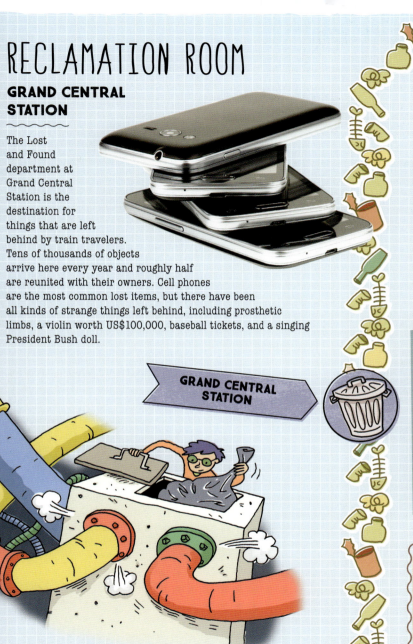

GRAND CENTRAL STATION

PROFESSOR OF TRASH

NYU (NEW YORK UNIVERSITY)

NYU is home to Professor Robin Nagle – official anthropologist in residence to the NY Department of Sanitation – whose role is to follow the workers around and learn their habits and language.

Here are a few of the garbage guys' special work words, as recorded by their personal professor:

FRUIT WAGON, SALAD WAGON, or **WHITE ELEPHANT** – a garbage truck.

HOPPER JUICE – the smelly liquid that builds up in a truck. Somebody eventually has to clean it out.

27

WASHINGTON STREET

TRASH TO ART
WASHINGTON STREET

NY artists often create work using recycled trash, and their sculptures spring up in parks and on street corners. An early example turned up in 1983 when artist H. A. Schult famously created an artwork called *Now* by turning the whole of Washington Street into a wastepaper river, using old copies of the *New York Times*. This photo shows an outfit made from recycled newsprint at the Trashion Fashion Show, held in NY in 2014 to showcase garbage-based fashion designs.

ABOUT 11,000 TONS OF RESIDENTIAL TRASH IS COLLECTED DAILY FROM NY HOMES.

FROM PILES TO PICNICS
FRESH KILLS, STATEN ISLAND

For a while, this 3.8-square-mile (9.9 sq km) landfill was the biggest in the world. In fact, its huge piles of New York trash made it one of the biggest man-made structures on the entire planet. It opened in 1947, and at its peak, was taking in over 14,000 tons of trash a day. Luckily, things are different now. It's no longer a landfill site – it has been reclaimed and turned into a huge beautiful park, where wildlife is welcome.

STATEN ISLAND

WIPE, FLUSH, BLOCK!
NEWTON CREEK

Newton Creek hosts the city's biggest sewage treatment plant, but they say the NY sewage system is under siege... by wet wipes! They clog the system and sometimes mix with waste grease to create a kind of "fatberg" – a big block of barf-inducing gunk that's very hard to budge. NY has recently had to spend US$18 million or more trying to solve the problem, which is why New Yorkers are being asked to think before they flush their wipes.

NEWTON CREEK

ATTACK ON RATS
ALL OVER TOWN!

New York has declared war on its rats. Currently there's around one rat for every four people, but the city is spending millions on getting rid of the beastly disease-spreading furballs. A "rat squad" of inspectors target rat hotspots called "rat reservoirs" – locations such as sewers and parks where most of the rats live.

ALL OVER TOWN!

search: NYC TRASH FACTS

- **1.3 BILLION GALLONS** (4.9 billion liters) of water produced daily in NY.
- **1,300 TONS** of "biosolids" (organic material in sewage) processed daily.
- **6,000 MILES** (9,656 km) – the length of NY's sewage pipes.

URBAN JUNGLE

Take a walk on the wild side to meet some of the unexpected and exotic critters that live alongside New York City's human inhabitants. Animals are all around town, if you just know where to look.

START

NIGHTTIME PROWLERS

VAN CORTLANDT PARK

If you hear a blood-curdling howl in the Bronx, don't assume it's coming from the zoo. Coywolves have been roaming New York City since the 1990s and they have made themselves at home in Van Cortlandt Park. These coyote-wolf crossbreeds have adapted well to life in the city, where they prey on mice, rats, rabbits, squirrels – and the occasional family pet!

SCALY ESCAPEE

BRONX ZOO

In 2011, one of the deadliest residents of the Bronx Zoo, a venomous Egyptian cobra, whose bite could kill a human in 15 minutes, escaped and made headlines around the world. While keepers searched for her, a Twitter account – @BronxZoosCobra – gave updates on her adventures as she (supposedly) slithered around the city. The fanged fugitive, who now has more than 166,000 Twitter followers, was found six days later, coiled in a corner of the reptile house!

BRONX ZOO

REPTILE HOME
TURTLE POND, CENTRAL PARK

Baby turtles make cute pets, but they're often abandoned when they grow to full size. Some have been dumped in Central Park and they've found a home in a small pool, now named Turtle Pond in their honor. Their new residence has everything they need. An island keeps them and their eggs safe from predators, and there are plenty of prime sunbathing spots, too.

THERE ARE FIVE DIFFERENT SPECIES OF TURTLE IN THE POND. THE MOST COMMON IS THE RED-EARED SLIDER, WHICH HAS SMALL RED SPOTS AROUND ITS EARS.

TURTLE POND, CENTRAL PARK

CATHEDRAL OF ST. JOHN THE DIVINE

BEASTLY BLESSINGS
CATHEDRAL OF ST. JOHN THE DIVINE

On the first Sunday of October, the Cathedral of St. John the Divine looks more like a petting zoo than a church. Each year, the "Blessing of the Animals" is held there to celebrate the Feast of St. Francis. Hundreds of creatures, including oxen, alpacas, miniature horses, sheep — and even a camel and a kangaroo — are led up to the altar to be blessed.

BEST BONES

AMERICAN MUSEUM OF NATURAL HISTORY

Famous paleontologists Barnum Brown and Henry F. Osborn traveled the world to collect dinosaur bones, then brought the best back to New York. Thanks to them, the American Museum of Natural History (AMNH) has the largest collection of dinosaur bones in the world.

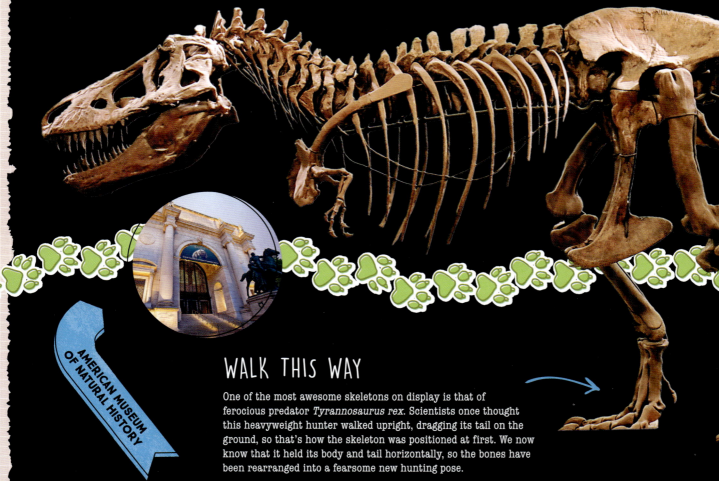

AMERICAN MUSEUM OF NATURAL HISTORY

WALK THIS WAY

One of the most awesome skeletons on display is that of ferocious predator *Tyrannosaurus rex*. Scientists once thought this heavyweight hunter walked upright, dragging its tail on the ground, so that's how the skeleton was positioned at first. We now know that it held its body and tail horizontally, so the bones have been rearranged into a fearsome new hunting pose.

6 IN. (15 CM) LENGTH OF **TOOTH**

5 FT. (1.5 M) LENGTH OF **SKULL**

40 FT. (12 M) LENGTH FROM NOSE TO TAIL

REX'S SECRETS

The bones that make up the *T. rex* skeleton in the AMNH are almost all real fossils, but they come from two different dinosaurs, both discovered in Montana. The *T. rex* also has two heads! The skeleton has a lightweight fake head, and the real skull is on display nearby. It's too heavy to put on the bones!

85 PERCENT OF THE SKELETONS AT THE AMNH ARE MADE UP OF REAL FOSSILIZED BONES.

NEAR NY

No dino bones have ever been unearthed in New York State, but we know dinosaurs must have lived here because footprints were discovered in Rockland County, close to NYC. There have been lots of finds in nearby New Jersey, too, including the footprints of a large meat-eater!

DINO DELIGHT

UP ON THE FOURTH FLOOR THERE ARE MORE THAN 600 COMPLETE OR NEAR-COMPLETE SKELETONS OF DINOSAURS AND OTHER PREHISTORIC REPTILES AND MAMMALS. MUSEUMS OFTEN USE PLASTER CASTS TO REPLACE THE MISSING BONES IN INCOMPLETE SKELETONS.

search: GOVERNORS ISLAND

MILITARY BASE

For 200 years the island was a military base, but in 2003 most of the land was sold to the people of New York.

360° VIEW

In 2014, "the hills" there were constructed out of recycled materials. They provide visitors with a 360-degree view, taking in the Statue of Liberty, New York Harbor, and the Lower Manhattan skyline.

MYSTERY SOLVED
GOVERNORS ISLAND

When bees on Governors Island started to produce bright red honey, their keepers were baffled. The cause was finally discovered at Dell's Maraschino Cherries Company in nearby Red Hook. The bees had been feasting on the sugar syrup used to make cocktail cherries, which contains a red dye. When lids were fitted to the vats of syrup, the honey went back to its normal color.

GOVERNORS ISLAND

RADIO CITY MUSIC HALL

ANIMAL ACT
RADIO CITY MUSIC HALL, ROCKEFELLER CENTER

If you spot a camel strolling down Sixth Avenue in November or December, you're not imagining things. Along with sheep and a donkey, camels are the furry co-stars of the "Living Nativity," one of the highlights of Radio City's famous Christmas Spectacular stage show.

THE NEW YORK AQUARIUM OPENED IN 1896, AND IS THE OLDEST CONTINUALLY RUNNING AQUARIUM IN THE US.

SANDY SURVIVORS
NEW YORK AQUARIUM

At the New York Aquarium you can come face-to-fin with thousands of sea-dwellers. The aquarium was badly damaged back in 2012, when it was flooded by Hurricane Sandy. Most of the creatures stayed safely in their tanks, but a baby walrus was later found happily swimming through the storm waters, and an eel was discovered in a shower stall.

CITY SQUAWKERS
GREEN-WOOD CEMETERY

The residents of most cemeteries are a quiet bunch, but that's not true of Brooklyn's Green-Wood Cemetery. A noisy colony of monk parakeets have built their untidy nests here among the historic monuments. These exotic birds might look out of place during a freezing New York winter, but they normally live in southern Argentina where frost and snow are common. The parakeets are thought to have escaped from a shipping crate while in transit at a New York airport in the 1960s.

NY AQUARIUM

GREEN-WOOD CEMETERY

GOING UNDERGROUND

There are many miles of underground tunnels beneath New York, some of them hiding surprising secrets. It's time to turn on your flashlight and discover what's down there!

MOO MYSTERY
12TH AVENUE

New York has lots of tunnels, but does it have one for cows? Some say there is a lost cattle tunnel on the West Side, somewhere under 12th Avenue. Cattle were once brought into the Meatpacking District via barge from New Jersey, and the story goes that the tunnel was built to stop them causing cow-jams in the local streets. It's referred to in old books and newspapers, and is even marked on plans, but nobody knows for sure whether it's a moo-myth or the real deal!

CITY HALL OLD STATION

LOST LAND OF TRAINS
CITY HALL OLD STATION

This beautiful station opened in 1904, closed in 1945, and is now a secret subway spot. Travelers can only see it when it's open for tours, or if they stay on a downtown six train as it loops around after Brooklyn Bridge station. The station is stunning, with beautiful tiles, skylights, and pretty chandeliers – so it's no surprise that its designers also built cathedrals.

58 JORALEMON ST.

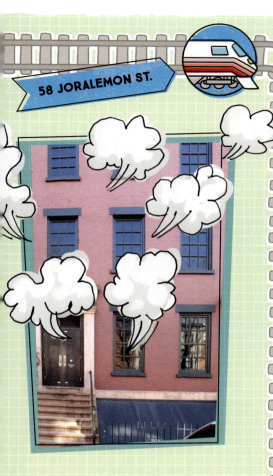

STATION SHOW
UNION SQUARE STATION

This is known as the best location for buskers in the subway, though they perform all over the system. For many years busking was banned as a noise nuisance, but in 1985 it was made legal again. Entertainers can now audition every year to get preferential spots to play or sing for the public. Some of the subway musicians have gone on to careers aboveground in theaters and concert halls. Travelers should be on the lookout for the next big noise playing in a tunnel near them!

UNION SQUARE STATION AND OTHER LOCATIONS

SECRET PORTAL HERE!
58 JORALEMON ST.

This may look like a smart townhouse, but nobody's ever home because it's not a house at all. It's a craftily disguised air vent and emergency exit for the New York subway, nine stories below. Few people have seen inside. Those that have been granted access say it's a weird empty space filled with walkways.

 7,500 NUMBER OF OFFICIAL WEEKLY BUSKING PERFORMANCES ON THE NY SUBWAY

 30 OFFICIAL BUSKING SITES ON THE NY SUBWAY

search: NYC SUBWAY ART

STYLES

NYC's subway art comes in all shapes, sizes, and styles. It includes:

- mosaic murals
- famous quotes
- stained glass
- nautical charts
- photography
- sound installations

CHRISTOPHER JANNEY ALSO CREATED A TEMPORARY "SOUNDSTAIR" INSTALLATION ON THE STEPS OF NYC'S METROPOLITAN MUSEUM. THE STEPS PLAYED MUSICAL NOTES AS PEOPLE STOOD ON THEM.

14TH ST. / 8TH AVE.

ART PEOPLE UNDERGROUND

14TH ST. / 8TH AVE.

There's some great art on display down in the subway, and one of the most popular examples is *Life Underground*, by Tom Otterness. His little figures pop up where you least expect them – sitting by commuters, crawling along railings, or climbing up walls. They've become underground favorites because they raise a subway smile.

SOUNDS GREAT!

34TH ST. HERALD SQUARE

A long green box suspended above the platforms here allows travelers to play beautiful music while they're waiting for a train. It's an art installation called *REACH*, by Christopher Janney. Anyone who waves a hand in front of one of its eight eyes breaks a beam of light and is rewarded with sounds ranging from melodic musical instruments to soothing moods from nature, such as birdsong or raindrops.

34TH ST. HERALD SQUARE

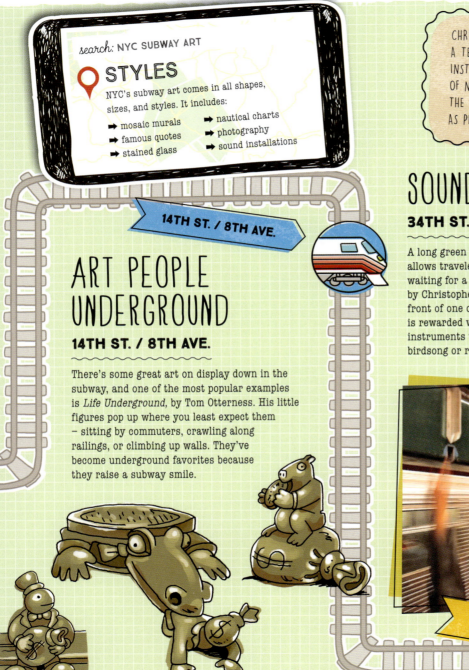

TIME-TRAVEL HERE
NY TRANSIT MUSEUM, COURT STREET

The entrance looks like a normal subway station, but inside it's a celebration of subway history. Visitors love to hop on and off the vintage subway cars kept here, and travel back in time to 1904, when the first subway opened. On that opening day, more than 100,000 excited New Yorkers paid a nickel for their ride, and the city's mayor took the train controls for the very first run.

NY TRANSIT MUSEUM, COURT STREET

Subway

The subway is such an important feature of New York City, it deserves its own special "stop," a place to knock your socks off with its incredible stats. So finish your trail and take a seat for a NY-style numbers ride...

5.6 MILLION

Around 5.6 million people travel daily on the subway.

That's around 1.751 billion people a year. (It's the 7th-biggest subway in the world. Beijing takes the top spot.)

39,000

There are 39,000 sidewalk ventilation grates allowing air in and out.

361 MILLION MILES

The subway car fleet travels around 361 million miles (581 million km) a year between 468 station stops.

If you laid all the transit train tracks end to end, they would stretch from New York to Chicago.

There are 72 bridges and 14 under-river tunnels, called "tubes."

39

BITE INTO THE BIG APPLE

If you're feeling hungry, you're in luck. New York is like a giant table laden with foods from around the world, so no wonder it has a foodie-style nickname – the Big Apple! Get ready to feast on this trail of treats.

PIZZA HEAVEN
LOMBARDI'S, 32 SPRING ST.

In the late 1800s, Italian immigrants from Naples brought with them their love of Naples-style pizza. Gennaro Lombardi opened New York's first pizzeria in 1905, adapting his Italian baking techniques to create the New York pizza. He catered to local tastes by cooking in coal-fired ovens and using mozzarella from cow's milk (in Naples they used buffalo milk and powered their ovens with wood). We salute Gennaro and his baker colleagues for over 100 years of delicious NY pizza. *Bellissimo!*

BROOKLYN

BEST BAGELS
BROOKLYN

Originally from Europe, the recipe for bagels was brought to the US by immigrants, and was once a closely guarded secret. Good bagels have a crunchy skin and are soft on the inside, but Brooklyn's bagel-makers claim theirs are the best in the world, due to the water. Brooklyn's water comes all the way from the Catskill Mountains 256 miles (412 km) away, and contains a special blend of minerals. Bagel-makers have analyzed the Brooklyn water and re-created its mineral mix in bagel-making all over the US.

SPRING STREET

PERFECT PICKLES
THE PICKLE GUYS, 49 ESSEX ST.

People come from miles around to pick perfect pickles from The Pickle Guys. These guys pickle in barrels, using salty water, garlic, and spices, and are the last pickle vendor left in the Lower East Side's pickle district. All kinds of goodies are on sale here, from pickled tomatoes and sauerkraut to seasonal treats, such as pickled pineapple. Around Passover, they cater to the Jewish community by grating fresh horseradish from morning until night for days, which is then used in Passover meals. The employee who does it wears a gas mask!

ESSEX STREET

PIZZA STATS!
- There are over **9,000** pizzerias in NYC.
- **350** slices of pizza are eaten **every second** across the **US**. There goes another 350!
- The whole of America celebrates the succulent slice during **National Pizza Week** in **January**.

BAYARD STREET

NICE AND ICY
CHINATOWN ICE-CREAM FACTORY, 65 BAYARD ST.

The origins of ice cream go way back into the frozen mists of time. Some say it was the Chinese who first came up with this cool creation thousands of years ago. We'll never know who took the first lovely lick, but we do know that New York has its own Chinese maestro ice-cream store – the Chinatown Ice-Cream Factory. Here, Chinese flavors, such as lychee, mango, red bean, and durian fruit, are served in cones and cups made of black sesame seeds.

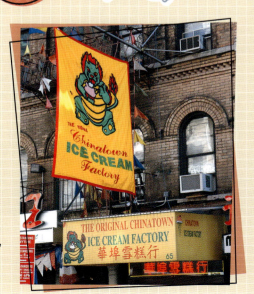

WHO INVENTED THE ICE-CREAM CONE? FOODIES ARGUE OVER THIS FOR HOURS, BUT WE KNOW FOR SURE THAT ONE OF THE VERY FIRST PIONEERS WAS NEW YORKER ITALO MARCHIONY, WHEN HE BEGAN SELLING ICE-CREAM CUPS MADE FROM WAFFLES SHAPED INTO BOWLS.

LET'S GO LATIN
RED HOOK BALL FIELDS

Part of the fun in going to watch sporting events is trying the snacks from vendors on the sidelines, right? At Red Hook Ball Fields, people go to play baseball, but also to try the Latin-American selection of track-side chow from the local food trucks. Empanadas, tamales, and pupusa are among the Latin dishes that feature here (a pupusa is a pancake-type patty from El Salvador, filled with all kinds of delicious cheesy mixtures). We could go on, but we're beginning to feel too hungry. Tacos, anyone?

RED HOOK BALL FIELDS

THE GRANDDADDY OF DELIS
KATZ'S DELI, 205 E. HOUSTON STREET

How big can a sandwich be? Katz's pastrami ones are enormous. Here, they make their own pastrami the gourmet way, and it takes 30 days to cure the mouthwatering meat. Katz is the granddaddy of delis because it's the oldest in New York, first founded in 1888. Among other delicious goodies, it serves around 10,000 pounds (4,500 kg) of pastrami every week. So, since 1888, that's... well, let's just say it's a lot of meat and a lot of sandwiches!

search: NEW YORK DELIS

DELICATESSEN

The word "deli" is short for "delicatessen" – a word meaning "fine foods."

German immigrants first introduced delicatessens to New York. The city is now world famous for delis from many different cultures – especially Jewish and Italian.

E. HOUSTON STREET

42

CREAMY AND DREAMY
JUNIOR'S DELI, 368 FLATBUSH AVENUE

People have been eating different kinds of cheesecake for centuries. Even the Ancient Romans had their own version, using ricotta mixed with honey. Then, in 1872, a farmer in Chester, New York, created cream cheese while experimenting with milk and started a cheesecake revolution! The cream cheese version we know and love today was soon born — and New York foodies say the best slices are found at Junior's. Here, they leave the cheesecake for 48 hours before serving it, to age the flavor to perfection.

FLATBUSH AVE.

35TH STREET

SWEET-TREAT STREET
FACTORY, 68 35TH STREET

Even the air smells of chocolate in New York's oldest chocolate-making spot. Chocolates have been handmade by the Li-Lac company since 1923, and some of the original recipes are still used today. There's almond bark, caramel squares, butter crunch, salted caramels, walnut caramel bars, coconut clusters, chocolate strawberries... enough already! The company also owns over 1,000 molds for making all kinds of chocolate shapes. They've even made life-sized violins and shoes, and the Society of Neurosurgeons once ordered 13,000 chocolate brains.

CONEY ISLAND

FUN IN A BUN

NATHAN'S HOT-DOG-EATING CONTEST, SURF AND STILLWELL AVENUES

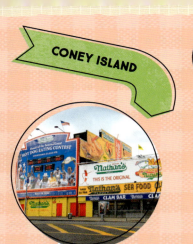

Every July 4, one of the world's most prestigious eating contests takes place in Coney Island, on the pennisula of southwestern Brooklyn, New York City. The fastest hot-dog eaters on the planet converge here for the honor of eating as many hot dogs as they can in 10 minutes in front of a crowd of 50,000 or more and a big TV audience. Beforehand, they have a weigh-in with the mayor, and then arrive on board the "bus of champions."

PRO-EATING LOWDOWN

The event is run by the International Federation of Competitive Eating, and the contestants sign a contract with the organization, just like wrestlers sign a contract with WWE (World Wrestling Entertainment). They take part in other events, too, such as burger- and pizza-eating contests, and are ranked in a league.

44

BARFING BANNED!

The competitors have to eat as many hot dogs with buns as they can (no leaving those buns!). They're allowed to dunk the dogs in water if it helps, and each person has their own scorer who keeps a tally of their progress. They get penalties for messy eating and if they vomit, they are disqualified. If there's a tie, there's a hot dog eat-off.

TRUE CHAMPIONS

US superstar Joey Chestnut won the contest for eight years, with a record of 69 hot dogs in 10 minutes. Japanese munching master Takeru Kobayashi (above) won six times in a row. Sonya Thomas (left) is the top female winner, and is the most successful food-eating star of all. This tiny lady holds around 39 world-eating records – including the Nathan's hot dog women's record of 45 in 10 minutes. The winners are awarded a jeweled belt – mustard-colored for men and pink for women.

70 ESTIMATED NUMBER OF **HOT DOGS** EACH AMERICAN EATS IN ONE YEAR

20 BILLION ESTIMATED NUMBER OF **HOT DOGS** EATEN AT US SPORTING EVENTS, CARNIVALS, AND FAIRS IN **ONE YEAR**

CARTS COST

There are around 150 food-vending carts licensed to sell in New York's parks, providing hot dogs, water, snow cones, toasted nuts, etc. Vendors have to buy a license to be there, and the ones in Central Park cost over US$200,000 a year. That's a lot of hot dogs to sell. Send over Joey Chestnut and Sonya Thomas!

TOP TREASURES

New York has some of the finest museums and art galleries in the world, with many famous objects on show. Step this way for a display of hidden and not-so-hidden delights, brought together in one place for the very first time.

THE MORGAN LIBRARY

THE EVERYTHING MUSEUM
THE CITY RELIQUARY

This cosy community museum is run by local people, and features "treasures" from everyday New York life. There's everything here, from old baseball tickets to vintage bottles and a dentist's chair. Recent treats include a display about the history of doughnuts and a fascinating exhibition on everything to do with chickens.

WORLD'S FIRST WRITING
THE MORGAN LIBRARY

John Pierpont Morgan was a fabulously successful banker who also collected things. When Morgan died in 1924, his son gave his father's grand library to the public. It houses famous first-edition books, drawings by the world's greatest artists, and also a collection of tiny treasures – little seals around 1 inch (2.5 cm) long, engraved with pictures and symbols. They may look insignificant, but some are 5,000 years old, and they're among the very first examples of written symbols in the world.

THE CITY RELIQUARY

START

46

NEW YORK PUBLIC LIBRARY

TOP TEDDY BEAR
NEW YORK PUBLIC LIBRARY

Once upon a time, a little boy called Christopher Robin Milne was given a teddy bear by his mom, along with some other cuddly little friends – Piglet, Eeyore, Tigger, and Kanga. Watching him play, his writer dad, A. A. Milne, got ideas for stories about the bear, named Winnie-the-Pooh. Soon the character had become world famous. The original toys found their way to New York, where they now sit in a library basement room, behind bulletproof glass.

IN 2008, TIFFANY'S CREATED A CELL PHONE FEATURING MORE THAN 400 DIAMONDS. ONLY TEN WERE MADE.

THE BLING BUILDING
TIFFANY'S

Every New Yorker knows where Tiffany's is. Since 1940, this iconic store has been selling sparkling jewels to everyone from royalty and movie stars to ordinary folk looking for the perfect present. It's also the home of the Tiffany Yellow Diamond (above) – one of the largest ever found. Worth around US$12 million, it's been made into a necklace with diamonds and platinum.

TIFFANY'S

47

MINI-MILLIONS
METROPOLITAN MUSEUM OF ART

The Met is the biggest museum in the western hemisphere, and over 6 million people visit each year. It's stuffed with treasures of all kinds, but one in particular might surprise you more than most. It's a little painting measuring just 11 inches (27.9 cm) by 8.75 inches (21.18 cm). The frame is even damaged with burn marks from candles lit under it long ago. Why is it so special? It's *Madonna and Child*, by Duccio di Buoninsegna, and it's the most expensive object in the entire museum, valued at US$45 million!

THE PAINTING *MADONNA AND CHILD* IS OVER 700 YEARS OLD.

STOLEN SAPPHIRE
AMERICAN MUSEUM OF NATURAL HISTORY

The world's biggest blue star sapphire, the Star of India, lives here, protected by the latest hi-tech security. But it wasn't always so safe. Back in 1964, two Miami robbers discovered that nobody had replaced the museum's alarm batteries, so they broke in through an open window. The thieves snatched the sapphire, along with a haul of jewels, but when they got back to Miami they celebrated too loudly and were caught. They had hidden the sapphire in a locker at a Miami bus station!

THE STAR OF INDIA SAPPHIRE IS ONE OF THE OLDEST TREASURES IN NEW YORK CITY. IT'S AROUND 2 BILLION YEARS OLD AND WAS DISCOVERED IN SRI LANKA.

UNDER WRAPS
SECRET LOCATIONS MIDTOWN

Where do New York's museums put their spare treasures? It turns out that some top museums and galleries keep their excess collections hidden away in Midtown Manhattan, in areas such as Chelsea and the Upper East Side. Those in the know say these secret stores have the latest security, and special fire, temperature, and humidity controls to keep the art safe – but there's no hint on the outside of the buildings as to what's inside.

GET DIGGING!
LONG ISLAND

Here's a New York treasure that's still to be found! Notorious pirate Captain Kidd once skulked around town until he was caught by the British and hanged back in London in 1701. He was said to be a wealthy man from his career in piracy, but he went to his death without revealing the locations of his hidden treasure stashes. One hoard was found on Gardener's Island, but more booty is thought to be still buried somewhere on Long Island.

SECRET LOCATIONS MIDTOWN

search: **CAPTAIN KIDD**

📍 **A LIFE AT SEA**
Captain William Kidd was born in Dundee, Scotland, in 1654 and took to the sea when he was just a boy.

📍 **PRIVATEER**
He began his career as a privateer – a kind of "legal" pirate, hired by governments to attack foreign ships.

LONG ISLAND

IT'S SHOWTIME!

Lights! Curtains! It's time to set the stage for a tour of some of New York's great theaters, starting with its world-renowned Theater District. Get your tap shoes tapping to start the show.

THEATER CENTRAL

BROADWAY

It's every actor's dream to be on Broadway. It's the magical heart of US theater, the street where stars are made on stage. The theatrical route runs right through Manhattan, but it's so old it was an ancient pathway before the city was even founded.

BROADWAY

search: NEW YORK STAGE STATS

BROADWAY
There are around 40 theaters on Broadway.

TICKET SALES
Broadway shows make more than US$1 billion in ticket sales in a year.

TIMES SQUARE

The heart of Broadway is Times Square, where every business has an illuminated sign. Each year there's a big New Year celebration here. Everyone looks up at the famous shining ball mounted on a flagpole on top of a roof. The ball begins to drop at 11.59 and comes to rest at the bottom at exactly midnight. Happy New Year!

BRIGHT LIGHTS

Broadway's nickname is "The Great White Way" because the billboards and theaters shine bright lights up into the night sky. It was one of the first streets in the entire US to get electric lights, way back in 1880.

THIEVES STREET

Long ago, in the 1800s, this area had a nickname – Thieves Lair – because it was the haunt of pickpockets. Goats and pigs also roamed around back then among the tumbledown shanties of the poor. When the planners arrived to develop the street, a local Dutch tavern-keeper refused to let them cut down his favorite tree, which is why the street swerves to the west instead of going straight.

THE PHANTOM OF THE OPERA IS BROADWAY'S LONGEST RUNNING SHOW. IT BEGAN IN 1988.

YOU WON THE WEIGHT!

EACH YEAR, THE BEST BROADWAY STARS AND SHOWS WIN TONY AWARDS, NAMED AFTER BROADWAY ACTRESS AND THEATER-FOUNDER ANTOINETTE PERRY. THE AWARD CONSISTS OF A MEDALLION MOUNTED ON A BASE. IN 2010, THE BASE WAS MADE HEAVIER AND BIGGER, SO IT LOOKED AND FELT MORE IMPRESSIVE. IT WAS ALWAYS A BIG DEAL TO WIN A TONY, BUT NOW IT'S LITERALLY AN EVER BIGGER DEAL!

THE NEW VICTORY THEATER DOESN'T JUST PUT ON PLAYS. IT SHOWCASES DANCE, CIRCUS, OPERA, AND MUSIC FROM AROUND THE WORLD, TOO.

MRS. GHOST
NEW VICTORY THEATER

The New Victory is the oldest theater still operating in NY, and it's dedicated to kids, putting on fantastic child-friendly shows. Apparently it's got a ghost, too, but she's a friendly one. They say it's the ghost of Mrs. Leslie Carter, once a famous New York actress. Musicians at the theater often accuse her of messing with their instruments, twiddling the knobs and strings and even playing them overnight when nobody is there to hear!

NEW VICTORY THEATER

DANCE!
MTV STUDIOS

MTV STUDIOS

New York dancers like to make an impact with their performances, and in 2015 performers outside the MTV Studios got into the *Guinness Book of Records* for the world's longest dance-relay marathon. They had a "Beyoncéthon," dancing to Beyoncé's music for over 24 hours and 9 minutes. Another world record was set in 2014 in Herald Square, when a record 406 people boogied together.

IT MUST BE CHRISTMAS
LINCOLN CENTER

Every Christmas in New York a little girl has a dream about her favorite Christmas toy, the Nutcracker Prince. He comes alive and defeats the evil Mouse King, then takes her to the magical Land of Snow, where the Sugar Plum Fairy dances for her. That's the story of the classic *Nutcracker* ballet, performed here every year since 1954 by the New York City Ballet, America's biggest dance troupe.

LINCOLN CENTER

SCHOOL FOR STARS
JUILLIARD SCHOOL, LINCOLN CENTER

It's reputedly the best place in the world to learn performing arts, which is why it's so hard to get into this school of drama and music. Many musical and acting superstars have studied their craft here before making it big. The teachers here are famously tough on their students, to make them the best of the best at the box office. Musical prodigies can start taking Saturday classes here from the age of seven.

JUILLIARD SCHOOL, LINCOLN CENTER

CENTRAL PARK

OUTDOOR ACTING
DELACORTE THEATER, CENTRAL PARK

Every summer, theater-lovers vie for free tickets to see top actors perform Shakespeare plays outdoors at the Delacorte Theater in Central Park. Some top Hollywood stars have performed here, including Meryl Streep, Al Pacino, and Denzel Washington. In Shakespeare's time, over 400 years ago, the plays were acted in a theater with an open roof. Back then, the audience sometimes smelled so bad in hot weather they were nicknamed "stinkards." Luckily for the Delacorte crowd, deodorant has since been invented!

PUPPETS IN THE PARK
SWEDISH COTTAGE, CENTRAL PARK

There's a little piece of Sweden nestling in Central Park – a Swedish cottage that arrived here in 1877. Since 1947, it's been home to some very special actors and actresses... with strings! The Marionette Theatre performs fairy tales, such as *Jack and the Beanstalk* and *Peter Pan*, here, and it's brought puppet magic to hundreds of thousands of city children.

SWEDISH COTTAGE WAS ONCE USED AS HEADQUARTERS FOR CIVIL DEFENSE DURING WORLD WAR II.

SWEDISH COTTAGE, CENTRAL PARK

Many world-famous performers started out their career at the Apollo Theater in Harlem, including Michael Jackson, Elton John, and Stevie Wonder.

YOU'RE IN THIS, TOO!
IMMERSIVE THEATER, VARIOUS LOCATIONS

Immersive theater is when the audience joins in, and it's getting more and more popular in NY. Performances take place in unusual buildings rather than theaters, and if you go, you don't get a seat. Instead, the audience explores the building, meeting all kinds of characters and talking to them along the way. In recent times, audiences have been invited to help solve a murder, walk through a weird wonderland, and even join in a musical.

THE TOUGHEST IN TOWN
APOLLO THEATER

Anyone starting out with an act can audition at the famous talent contest in Harlem's Apollo Theater. The only trouble is the audience is notoriously tough and boos performers that it doesn't like. When the booing gets too loud, a siren goes off and "the Executioner" arrives to take the poor performer off the stage.

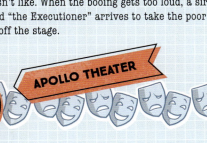

APOLLO THEATER

IMMERSIVE THEATER, VARIOUS LOCATIONS

WAY TO GO

This trail will transport you around New York in no time. There's a choice of pedal-power, horse-power, the bus, and the train... or you can even take one of New York's famous cabs. Let's go!

TAKING SIDES ON RIDES
CENTRAL PARK

Horse-drawn carriages have been part of the Central Park scene since the 1880s, when New Yorkers would take a ride through the park to escape the city streets. Now they're a major tourist attraction, but they're also very controversial. Some say it's cruel to use working horses in a city. Others say it's not. It's a big NY issue, with everyone having their say about the city's resident horses.

TAXI!
ALL OVER NEW YORK

Want to be a New York cab driver? First you'll need to pass a test, showing you know enough about traffic laws and map reading. Then you'll need to pay for a medallion. Look on the hood of a New York yellow cab and you will see the metal shield that shows it has a licence to operate. There are fewer than 14,000 medallions available, and they get bought and sold for a lot of money – up to US$1 million.

search: NY TAXI FACTS

600,000
The average number of cab passengers a day (236 million a year).

2.6 MILES (4.2 KM)
The average distance for a trip in a NY taxi.

485,000 APPROX. NUMBER OF NEW YORK **TAXI RIDES TAKEN IN ONE DAY**

175 MILLION APPROX. NUMBER OF NY TAXI RIDES TAKEN IN ONE YEAR

A TYPICAL CAB TRAVELS 70,000 MILES (112,654 KM) PER YEAR — THE EQUIVALENT OF 2.8 TIMES AROUND THE WORLD.

HARRY'S REVENGE
PLAZA HOTEL

When businessman Harry N. Allen was overcharged by a horse-drawn cab driver in 1907, he decided to start New York's first gasoline-powered cab service. He imported 65 red taxis from France, and lined them up in front of the brand-new Plaza Hotel. Later, the taxis were all painted yellow, after Harry learned that it's the color most easily seen from a distance.

GOING HOME
LONG ISLAND CITY

New Yorkers often complain that they can't get a taxi between four and five in the afternoon, and there's a reason for that. Most yellow cabs have two drivers, and this is the time they head across the Queensboro Bridge to change shifts. Most of the taxi garages, gas stations, and cab-driver training schools are in Long Island City.

PLAZA HOTEL

LONG ISLAND CITY

MEET YOU BY THE CLOCK
GRAND CENTRAL TERMINAL

The information booth at Grand Central Station is said to be the most popular place to meet up in New York. You can stand there watching some of the 750,000 people who cross the concourse daily, or perhaps take a look up at the clock on top of the booth, which has four faces made of opal and is worth around US$10 million. The staff at the information booth answers around 1,000 questions an hour.

CHECK OUT THESE BIG BUS STATS!

➡ **225,000 people** travel through the Port Authority Bus Terminal every weekday.

➡ Around **8,000 buses** leave from **223 departure gates** daily.

➡ Up to **66 million people** make **2.3 million departures** from here **every year!**

GRAND CENTRAL TERMINAL

THE PORT AUTHORITY BUS TERMINAL

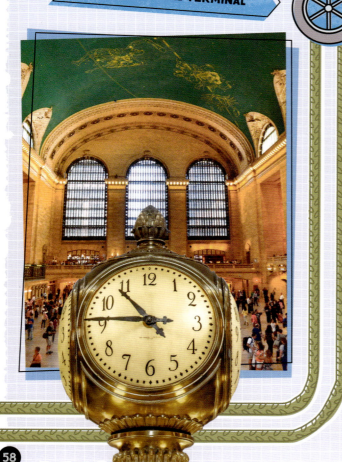

WORLD-BEATING BUSIEST
THE PORT AUTHORITY BUS TERMINAL

The Port Authority Bus Terminal is the largest in the US and the busiest in the world. Each year, long-suffering passengers give the Pokey Award (a golden snail) to the slowest bus service and the Schleppie Award (a pair of lumbering elephants) to the least reliable.

THERE ARE AN AVERAGE OF 34,176 CITI BIKE RIDES A DAY. ON AVERAGE, EACH BIKE IS RIDDEN EIGHT TIMES A DAY.

BIKE BALANCING ACT
CITI BIKE STATION, 33RD STREET AND 7TH AVENUE

New York's Citi Bike is the biggest bike rental system in the US, with 6,000 bikes and plans to double that number. The bike station at 33rd Street and 7th Avenue is the busiest in New York because it's close to Penn Station. Keeping popular stations stocked up is a real juggling act, and "rebalancers" are constantly moving bikes around the city on trailers.

CITI BIKE STATION

UNIVERSITY PLACE

TAKEN FOR A RIDE
UNIVERSITY PLACE

Japanese tourists Chisa and Hiroki Niwa got a shock when their pedicab (a pedal-powered taxi) dropped them off in University Place after a 20-minute ride. The normal price for their 39-block trip should have been around US$50, but the dishonest driver charged them US$720!

59

HARBOR TOUR

Come on board for a voyage around the shores of New York! We'll be sailing past shipwrecks, hidden gold, all kinds of ships (including a spaceship), and saltwater secrets before we reach the grandest lady in the US.

search: HUDSON RIVER

315 MILES (507 KM)
Length of the Hudson River

MUH-HE-KUN-NE-TUK
The Native American tribe of the Iroquois called the Hudson River Muh-he-kun-ne-tuk, meaning "the water that flows both ways," because it flows both north and south.

START

HUDSON LOWDOWN
HUDSON RIVER

The Hudson River was named after Henry Hudson, an Englishman who arrived to explore in 1609. It's been known to freeze over in hard winters, and in 1821 enterprising New Yorkers even ran pop-up taverns on the ice. Every year it hosts a race for tugboats, which also take part in strength contests, pushing each other nose-to-nose or stern-to-stern. For the spectators on the shore there's a popular spinach-eating contest.

SHIPWRECK SPOT
HELL'S GATE

This narrow tidal strait between Queens and Manhattan has some fearsome currents that have proved deadly to lots of vessels over the centuries. Its many shipwrecks include the British ship HMS *Hussar*, which sank in 1780. The rumor is that it was carrying millions of dollars' worth of gold! If so, the sunken treasure is still to be found...

ONE OF HMS *HUSSAR*'S CANNONS WAS FOUND AND DONATED TO CENTRAL PARK IN 1865. WORKERS CLEANING IT IN 2013, 148 YEARS LATER, FOUND IT WAS FULLY LOADED WITH GUNPOWDER AND A CANNONBALL READY TO FIRE!

HELL'S GATE

CITY SPACECRAFT
INTREPID SEA, AIR & SPACE MUSEUM

Fighter jets, spy planes, a missile-carrying submarine, a giant aircraft carrier, and even some spacecraft are all parked in New York! They're part of an exciting collection at the Intrepid Sea, Air & Space Museum at Pier 86. The space shuttle *Enterprise* is on show here. In 2012, it made a spectacular journey to the museum by barge, past the Statue of Liberty.

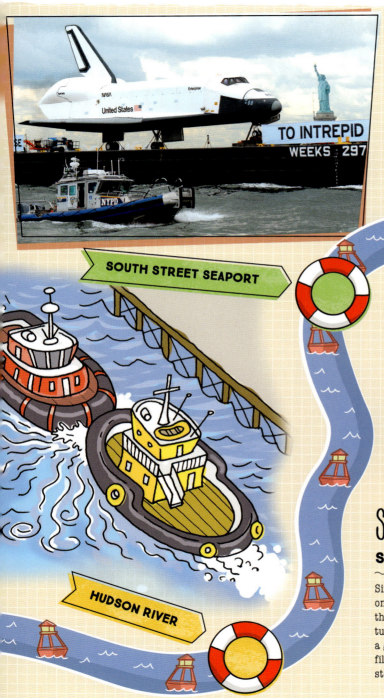

SHIPSHAPE SHIPS
SOUTH STREET SEAPORT

Six ships are on display here, including a floating lighthouse that once helped vessels avoid the treacherous sandbars waiting to run them aground in New York Bay. There's a sturdy steam-powered tugboat, a pretty fishing schooner, a grand old iron sailing ship, and a giant four-masted beauty called the *Peking*. She starred in a 1929 film, *Around Cape Horn*, which followed her progress in a huge storm off South America.

IT'S ELEPHANT-PROOF

BROOKLYN BRIDGE

When the Brooklyn Bridge was opened in 1883, it was the world's longest bridge. Local people were nervous. Would it be strong enough? A few days after it opened, a woman tripped down some stairs, someone cried out, and soon everyone on the bridge was panicking, thinking it was falling down. There was a fatal stampede, and 12 people died in the tragedy. The following year, circus owner P. T. Barnum led 21 elephants over the bridge to prove its strength. In fact, it's strong enough to withstand the weight of thousands of elephants.

135 FT. (41 M) HIGH AT CENTER

4 NUMBER OF MAIN CABLES

5,989 FT. (1,825 M) LENGTH

BROOKLYN BRIDGE

STINKY SWIM

GOWANUS CANAL

GOWANUS CANAL

This stretch of canal in South Brooklyn is said to be the most polluted waterway in the US. In 2015, environmentalist Chris Swain swam here to highlight the problem. He had to be decontaminated with bleach when he got out, and said it was "just like swimming in a dirty diaper." Plans are afoot to clean up the canal, but that won't be easy. It has more than 10 feet (3 m) of toxic sediment on the bottom, which locals call "black mayonnaise."

LADY OF THE LIGHT
ROBBINS REEF LIGHT

Robbins Reef Light is out in the waters between Manhattan Island and Staten Island. It's here that an unsung heroine called Katherine Walker became lighthouse keeper when her husband died in 1886. At 4 feet 10 inches (1.47 m), she was rather small, but she did a fantastic job until she retired at the age of 73. She kept the light burning and used her dinghy to rescue many sailors who were shipwrecked on the nearby reef. Once she even rescued a little Scottie dog and revived the poor pooch with coffee.

ROBBINS REEF LIGHT

IN THE DAYS BEFORE CARS, THE STATEN ISLAND FERRY TRANSPORTED HORSES BACK AND FORTH AS WELL AS PASSENGERS.

STATEN ISLAND

FERRY TO THE SAILORS
STATEN ISLAND

The only way to get to Staten Island is over the bridge from Brooklyn or on the free ferry that runs from Lower Manhattan. Around 65,000 passengers a day use the ferry. Once on Staten Island, visitors can go to the Sailors' Snug Harbor on the north shore. It's now a cultural center with peaceful gardens, but it got its name because it was once a home for "old, decrepit and worn-out" sailors. They don't sound all that decrepit, though. They were once known for their drunken fighting!

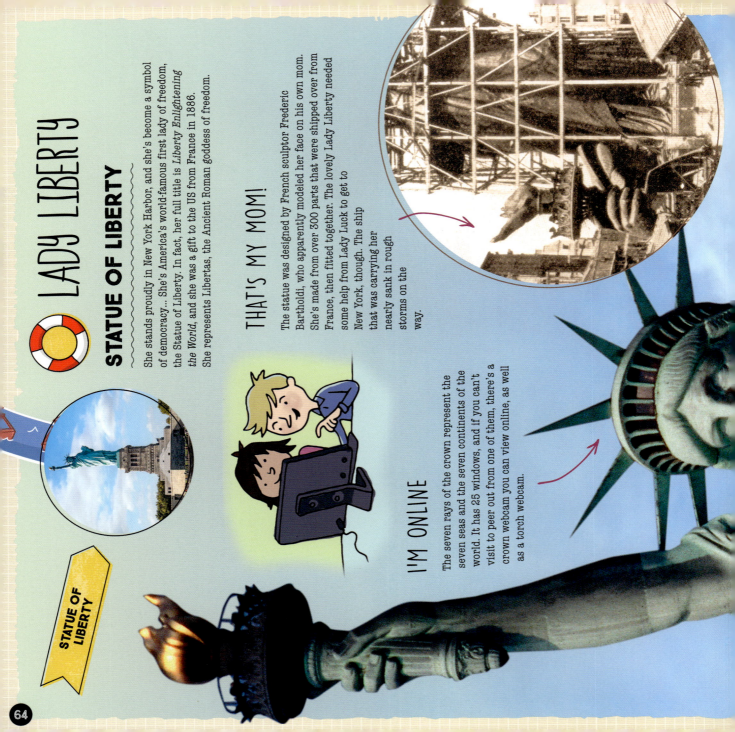

LADY LIBERTY

STATUE OF LIBERTY

She stands proudly in New York Harbor, and she's become a symbol of democracy... She's America's world-famous first lady of freedom, the Statue of Liberty. In fact, her full title is *Liberty Enlightening the World*, and she was a gift to the US from France in 1886. She represents Libertas, the Ancient Roman goddess of freedom.

THAT'S MY MOM!

The statue was designed by French sculptor Frederic Bartholdi, who apparently modeled her face on his own mom. She's made from over 300 parts that were shipped over from France, then fitted together. The lovely Lady Liberty needed some help from Lady Luck to get to New York, though. The ship that was carrying her nearly sank in rough storms on the way.

I'M ONLINE

The seven rays of the crown represent the seven seas and the seven continents of the world. It has 25 windows, and if you can't visit to peer out from one of them, there's a crown webcam you can view online, as well as a torch webcam.

STATUE OF LIBERTY

64

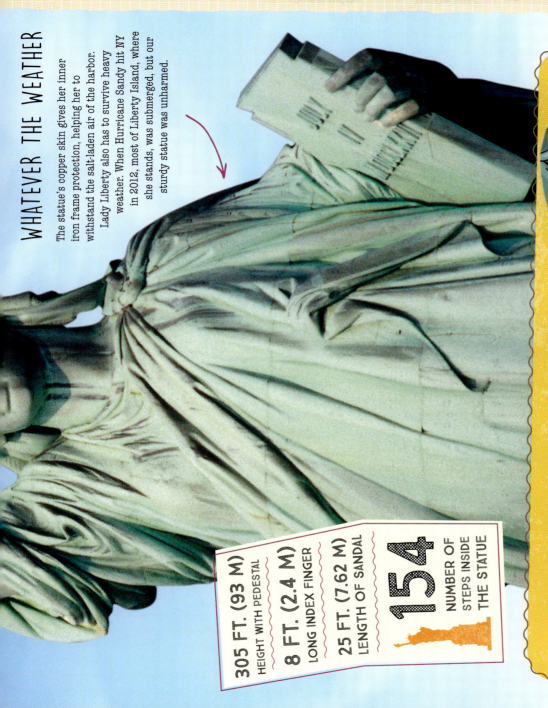

WHATEVER THE WEATHER

The statue's copper skin gives her inner iron frame protection, helping her to withstand the salt-laden air of the harbor. Lady Liberty also has to survive heavy weather. When Hurricane Sandy hit NY in 2012, most of Liberty Island, where she stands, was submerged, but our sturdy statue was unharmed.

305 FT. (93 M) HEIGHT WITH PEDESTAL

8 FT. (2.4 M) LONG INDEX FINGER

25 FT. (7.62 M) LENGTH OF SANDAL

154 NUMBER OF STEPS INSIDE THE STATUE

WHO KNOWS THIS?

Everyone can see that the statue carries a torch and a tablet (inscribed with the date of American Independence in Roman numerals). But it's a great quiz question to ask people what the statue has at her feet. Because it's a feature that's much harder to see. Partly hidden by her clothing, there's a broken chain, representing freedom from slavery.

65

FRIGHT FEST

Any city with a rich history is sure to be home to a few ghosts, but they say New York is the most haunted city in the US! No wonder they filmed the movie *Ghostbusters* here. Do you dare step onto this spooky trail?

MANHATTAN'S MOST HAUNTED

MERCHANT'S HOUSE MUSEUM

Now a museum, the Merchant's House has been called the "most haunted house in Manhattan." It was once the home of the Tredwell family, and Gertrude Tredwell, who died here in 1933, may still be keeping an eye on the place. Visitors and staff have reported mysterious piano music, flashing lights, unexplained smells, and sightings of a woman in a long, dress. So, someone is blaming smells on a spook? That sounds like a great new excuse for stinky socks!

THE MERCHANT'S HOUSE MUSEUM HAS BETWEEN SIX AND TWELVE REPORTS OF GHOSTLY GOINGS-ON EVERY YEAR.

THE HANGING TREE

WASHINGTON SQUARE PARK

The "Hangman's Elm" is over 330 years old, making it the oldest tree in NYC. According to legend, highwaymen were hanged from the tree and traitors were executed here during the American Revolution. There's no proof of this, but we do know that the park was once a "potter's field" – a burial ground for the poor. It's thought that the bodies of at least 20,000 people still lie beneath the grass and concrete.

MERCHANT'S HOUSE MUSEUM

WASHINGTON SQUARE PARK

WEST 10TH STREET

CROWDED HOUSE
14 WEST 10TH STREET

The pretty house at 14 West 10th Street has a surprising nickname – "House of Death." It's said to be haunted by no fewer than 22 of its past residents, including author Sam Clemens, better known as Mark Twain. A mother and daughter living there in the 1930s claimed to have seen him sitting by a window. According to them, he said: "My name is Clemens and I got problems here I gotta settle." Then he disappeared.

EERIE EATERY
ONE IF BY LAND, TWO IF BY SEA RESTAURANT, BARROW STREET

This restaurant was once a house belonging to US Vice President Aaron Burr (1756 to 1836). He and his daughter, Theodosia, are both said to haunt the place, along with up to 18 other ghosts from different time periods. Strange happenings include flying plates and chairs pulled from under customers. It's often described as New York's most romantic restaurant, so that could make for an awkward date! Theodosia is even suspected of removing customers' earrings at the bar.

AARON BURR IS A BUSY GHOST. HE'S ALSO BEEN SEEN HAUNTING THE MORRIS-JUMEL MANSION WHERE HE ONCE LIVED.

BARROW STREET

67

SPOOKY SCOTTIE
GRAND CENTRAL TERMINAL

Deep below Grand Central Terminal is a hidden platform with an elevator to the Waldorf-Astoria hotel above. It was used by President Franklin D. Roosevelt, who needed a wheelchair to get around. He wanted to keep his disability secret and this way he could sneak in and out without being seen. His Scottish terrier, Fala, was always at his side, and the dog's ghost is said to haunt tracks 112 and 113.

GRAND CENTRAL TERMINAL

MORRIS-JUMEL MANSION

TOLD OFF BY A GHOST
MORRIS-JUMEL MANSION

In 1964, a group of noisy schoolchildren were waiting to be let in to the Morris-Jumel Mansion when a woman on the balcony told them to be quiet. The students reported what had happened to the mansion's curator, who insisted the house was empty. The children later saw a portrait of Eliza Jumel, who had died in 1865, and recognized her as the woman on the balcony... Spooky, huh?

"Stop that noise!"

OTHER GHOSTS SPOTTED AT THE MORRIS-JUMEL MANSION INCLUDE A SOLDIER, A MAID, AND ELIZA JUMEL'S SECOND HUSBAND, AARON BURR (HE'S ALREADY HAUNTED THIS TRAIL ONCE!).

PUMPKIN PATCH
NEW YORK BOTANICAL GARDEN

When orange zombies, bats, and bugs start to appear at the New York Botanical Garden, you know it must be close to Halloween. The Haunted Pumpkin Garden opens from late September to the end of October. It combines spooky fun with creepy jack o'lanterns and other works of pumpkin art, all created by expert sculptors.

A COLOSSAL 2,058 LB. (933.5 KG) PUMPKIN, THE LARGEST EVER GROWN IN NORTH AMERICA, WAS ON DISPLAY AT THE NEW YORK BOTANICAL GARDEN IN OCTOBER 2014.

search: PUMPKIN CARVING

ANCIENT TRADITION

The Halloween pumpkin-carving tradition originated in Ireland. Children carved out turnips and potatoes and lit them with candles, as part of a Celtic religious festival. Later, Irish immigrants brought the tradition to America, home of the pumpkin.

 NEW YORK BOTANICAL GARDEN

 WOODLAWN CEMETERY

THE DEAD GO DOWNTOWN
WOODLAWN CEMETERY

The bodies of author Mark Twain and actress Olive Thomas lie among the grand tombs of Woodlawn Cemetery, but their ghosts apparently like to take a trip downtown. Mark Twain has been seen at his old home in Manhattan, and the beautiful Olive has been spotted more than once at the New Amsterdam Theater. She wears a green dress and holds the blue bottle of medicine that she accidentally drank in 1920, fatally poisoning herself.

GAME ON

With top teams in many major sports and some of the best venues in the world, New York has something for every sports fan. Step into your sneakers and take a jog around town to see who's scoring high.

THE NEW YORK METS' MASCOTS ARE MR. AND MRS. MET — A BASEBALL-HEADED COUPLE. THE NEW YORK JETS AND THE YANKEES DON'T HAVE MASCOTS. PITY!

ON YOUR MARK

STATEN ISLAND

On the first Sunday in November, more than 50,500 runners, wheelchair racers, and handcyclists gather in Fort Wadsworth to compete in the New York Marathon. When it began in 1970, the race was run in Central Park and just 55 people finished. Now it covers all five boroughs, and in 2015 there were 49,595 finishers.

MARATHON COMPETITOR DAVID BABCOCK KNITS AS HE RUNS TO RAISE MONEY FOR CHARITY. DURING THE 2014 NY RACE, HE KNITTED A SCARF WITH HIS FINGERS (NEEDLES WEREN'T ALLOWED). HE HOLDS THE WORLD RECORD FOR MARATHON SCARF-KNITTING, CREATING A SCARF OVER 12 FT. (3.65 M) LONG!

MEET THE MASCOTS

CONEY ISLAND

Mascot Sandy the Seagull welcomes fans to MCU Park, the home of minor-league baseball team the Brooklyn Cyclones. Each family-friendly game includes performances by the Beach Bums dance troupe and a race around the bases by three mascots dressed as hot dogs named Ketchup, Mustard, and Relish.

SUPERHERO SCHOOL
STREB LAB FOR ACTION MECHANICS (SLAM), BROOKLYN

Imagine a school where there are classes in flying through the air and walking up walls! Founded by dancer Elizabeth Streb, SLAM teaches young daredevils dance, free running, trapeze, and circus skills. It's all about getting fit and learning to use your muscles – great training for sports and dance, too.

WINNERS' WAY
CANYON OF HEROES, LOWER BROADWAY

New York likes to give its sporting stars a traditional ticker-tape parade – an avalanche of confetti as they ride in triumph through a section of lower Broadway nicknamed the "Canyon of Heroes." The women's national soccer squad was the first all-female team to be honored with a ticker-tape parade after winning the 2015 World Cup. Ticker tape was a type of paper ribbon produced by old-fashioned telegraph machines. Now shredded paper is used, but the name has stuck.

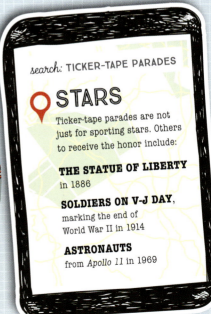

search: TICKER-TAPE PARADES

STARS

Ticker-tape parades are not just for sporting stars. Others to receive the honor include:

THE STATUE OF LIBERTY in 1886

SOLDIERS ON V-J DAY, marking the end of World War II in 1914

ASTRONAUTS from *Apollo 11* in 1969

MADISON SQUARE GARDEN

GRAND CENTRAL TERMINAL

COOL FLOOR
MADISON SQUARE GARDEN

This arena is home to both the NY Knicks basketball team and the NY Rangers ice hockey team. The ice rink is underneath the basketball court, covered by insulated material, so a quick change means it's possible to see a basketball game and a hockey game on the same day. The locker rooms are round to promote team unity. This way all the players can look each other in the eye! Out of respect, no one ever treads on the teams' giant logos on the locker-room floor.

"Duck!"

SHOWCASING SQUASH
GRAND CENTRAL TERMINAL

Each January, a huge glass-walled squash court is set up beneath the grand chandeliers of Vanderbilt Hall, Grand Central Terminal, ready for the annual Tournament of Champions. Spectators can sit within 10 feet (3 m) of the action and get a close-up view of the game as the ball flies towards the glass in front of their faces at up to 170 mph (274 km/h).

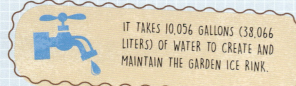

IT TAKES 10,056 GALLONS (38,066 LITERS) OF WATER TO CREATE AND MAINTAIN THE GARDEN ICE RINK.

THE ARTHUR ASHE STADIUM IS THE BIGGEST TENNIS VENUE IN THE WORLD.

COLORFUL COURTS
ARTHUR ASHE STADIUM

The Arthur Ashe Stadium is part of the Billie Jean King National Tennis Center, which hosts the US Open Grand Slam Tournament. It's named after the first African-American US Open champion. In 2005, the color of the center's artificial grass courts was changed from green to blue. Yellow is easier to see on a blue background than a green one, so the yellow tennis balls are now easier for players and TV viewers to spot.

ARTHUR ASHE STADIUM

BROOKLYN AND MANHATTAN

GO, GIRLS!
BROOKLYN AND MANHATTAN

Ever seen a roller derby? It's exciting and noisy, and some of the best action is to be found in NY, where the Gotham Girls' all-female league is based. The teams include the Queens of Pain, Brooklyn Bombshells, Manhattan Mayhem, Bronx Gridlock, the Wall Street Traitors, and the Grand Central Terminators. Young would-be rollers can start training with the Gotham Girls from the age of eight.

ROLLER DERBY RULES: TWO TEAMS ZOOM AROUND ON SKATES, AND EACH TEAM HAS A "JAMMER" — SOMEONE WHO SCORES POINTS BY LAPPING OPPOSING PLAYERS. THE REST OF THE TEAM CLEARS HER PATH OR TRIES TO BLOCK THE OPPOSING TEAM.

DIAMOND IN THE BRONX

YANKEE STADIUM

The New York Yankees are New York's Major League Baseball team. Yankee Stadium is their world-famous venue, but in 2009 they moved from the original building to a new site across the street. The new stadium cost US$2.3 billion, making it one of the most expensive sports venues ever built.

THE BRONX BOMBERS

The New York Yankees weren't always in New York, and they weren't always called the Yankees. The team was founded in 1901 in Baltimore, Maryland, under the name the Baltimore Orioles. They moved to New York in 1903 as the New York Highlanders, and didn't become the Yankees until 1913. They're nicknamed "The Bronx Bombers" because of their players' hitting power. They've had more famous players than you can swing a bat at, including Babe Ruth, Joe DiMaggio, Mickey Mantle, and Lou Gehrig.

A NEW ERA

The original 1923 stadium was nicknamed "The House That Ruth Built" after legendary player Babe Ruth. When he died in 1948, his body lay in state there and was viewed by more than 100,000 fans. The new stadium has been christened "The House That Jeter Built" after Derek Jeter, the Yankees' all-time top batter who retired in 2014.

US$2.3 BILLION
THE CALCULATED VALUE OF THE YANKEES TEAM IN 2013

1 MILLION+
ESTIMATED NUMBER OF HOT DOGS SOLD AT THE STADIUM IN ONE YEAR

1 NUMBER OF TOILETS PER **60** FANS

CHEERING AND JEERING

The "Bleacher Creatures" are a group of loud and loyal fans who strike fear into the opposing team. They always sit in the same spot and chant a roll call of the Yankees' players' names at the start of a game, until each player responds to the call. New player Hideko Matsui didn't know the rules, so his chant went on for two minutes before he acknowledged the Creatures!

HOME-RUN RIDDLE

In a game of baseball, one team tries to score by hitting the ball hard and running around the bases, while the other tries to prevent them from scoring. When the Yankees first switched stadiums, there was a sudden increase in home runs — when the ball sails straight over the outfield fence and the batter can run around all the bases in one play. Some people blamed the sharper angles of the outfield walls for creating a wind tunnel that lifted the ball over the fence. Since then, the number of home runs has fallen, and the cause remains a mystery.

SOUNDS GREAT!

Away from the car horns, sirens, and clatter of footsteps on the busy sidewalks, there are all sorts of unusual sounds around town. Keep your ears open as you explore this secret city soundscape.

HIP-HOP STOP
KOOL HERC'S HOUSE

In 1973, a teenager called Kool Herc started hosting parties in a community room in his Bronx high-rise home. He started using two turntables to loop beats... and that, so they say, was the birth of hip-hop! Lots of other sound-makers have followed Kool's creative lead, and there's still lots of innovative music going on in the area, from Latin and Afro-Cuban beats to rappers and beatboxers.

MUSIC, MAESTRO!
CARNEGIE HALL

Many great musicians and conductors have appeared on stage at this prestigious concert location, and Dr. Martin Luther King Jr. – the famous activist who led the Civil Rights movement in the US in the 1950s – spoke here in 1968. The building nearly disappeared around 1960, though, when there were plans to build a skyscraper on the site. Apart from the performances, there's something else you'll hear over and over again in Carnegie Hall. It's NYC's best-known joke: "How do you get to Carnegie Hall? Practice, practice, practice!"

SOUND VS. STORM
JANE'S CAROUSEL

This beautiful old carousel was built nearly 100 years ago and now it gives rides in Brooklyn Bridge Park. A bell chimes to start the ride, and the sounds of a fairground organ and drums accompany the horses as they prance around. These days, the carousel is enclosed in a glass box, which helped to save it when Hurricane Sandy hit Brooklyn in 2012. An eerie photo of the East River lapping up against the box, with the carousel lit up inside, trended worldwide. The picture became a symbol of local spirit in the face of the disaster. The carousel survived and plays on!

JANE'S CAROUSEL HAS 48 BEAUTIFUL, HAND-CARVED HORSES.

RHYMES AND CHIMES
DELACORTE CLOCK

Did you know there's a corner of Central Park where a hippo plays the violin and a penguin plays the drums? They're models on the musical Delacorte Clock in Central Park Zoo. When the clock chimes, the animals dance to nursery rhymes, along with a bear playing a tambourine, a mommy kangaroo playing a horn (her baby plays a mini-horn), a goat on panpipes, and an elephant with an accordion!

BEAT JAM
DRUMMER'S GROVE, PROSPECT PARK

A group of drummers began regularly meeting here in 1968, performing African-style. Soon other musicians and dancers followed, until eventually the site was officially named Drummer's Grove, and seats were provided for everyone to enjoy the jamming on Sunday afternoons. Since that first drumming session, the beats have been going on here for over 40 years!

WELCOME TO MY MUSIC
555 EDGECOMBE AVENUE

For over 20 years, Marjorie Eliot has held Sunday jazz sessions in her Harlem apartment. She puts out chairs in her kitchen, hallway, and parlor and anyone can come free of charge. The building she lives in is steeped in music. Famous singers and jazz musicians have lived there. Music must be in those bricks!

EDGECOMBE AVENUE

DRUMMER'S GROVE

search: DRUMMER'S GROVE

📍 BIG NOISE!

Around 400 drummers come to play at Drummer's Grove every Sunday. Their music permit only allows the musicians to drum until 7 o'clock in the evening, though, to avoid disturbing the local residents at night.

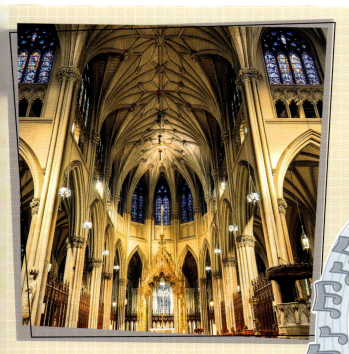

7 THE AVERAGE AGE THAT A MET ORCHESTRA MUSICIAN STARTED MUSIC LESSONS

9 THE AVERAGE AGE THAT A MET ORCHESTRA MUSICIAN TOOK UP THE INSTRUMENT THEY PLAY IN THE ORCHESTRA

METROPOLITAN OPERA HOUSE

THE MAGICAL MET
METROPOLITAN OPERA HOUSE

This is the largest opera house in the world, with 3,800 hi-tech seats. The back of each one is fitted with a screen to display a translation of the words for anyone who doesn't understand the original language of the opera. The Met has its own renowned orchestra, too, and it's released some stats (above) that might encourage you if you are trying to play a musical instrument! Keep going if you want to play here!

NAME THOSE BELLS
ST. PATRICK'S CATHEDRAL

There are 19 bells in St. Patrick's Cathedral, each one named after a Catholic saint. The bells include Bridget and Peter, Joseph and Michael, Agnes and Helena, and Alphonsus and Elizabeth. Patrick is the heaviest bell and Godfrey is the smallest. There were once bellringers, but these days the bells are played by electric keyboard. No two bells are the same, and each one plays a different note.

ST. PATRICK'S CATHEDRAL

79

BIG APPLE ART

In New York, art is all around and it often changes. There's creative inspiration to be found on almost every block, and you never know what you might see next. Take a tour of some arty highlights here.

MODERN MASTERS

THE MUSEUM OF MODERN ART

The Museum of Modern Art (MoMA) is one of the best-known art museums in the world, and it's packed with paintings by some of the most famous artists of recent times. It's home to works by, among others, Picasso, Dali, Matisse, Monet, Van Gogh, and Warhol.

MOMA

MORE THAN 150,000 WORKS OF ART

22,000 ORIGINAL FILMS

3 MILLION BOOKS

DARLING, I HATE IT!

One of the founders of MoMA was Abby Aldrich Rockefeller, the wife of John D. Rockefeller Jr., who built the Rockefeller Center. Although her husband was seriously rich, Abby had to raise the money for the museum herself because he hated modern art. When it opened in 1929, there were just six rooms and nine pieces of art, which were all gifts.

US$118 MILLION

SEEING SERIOUS MONEY

Flag, by Jasper Johns, on show at MoMA, is said to be the third most expensive painting on public display anywhere in the world. It's worth around US$118 million. It's beaten only by *The Scream*, by Edvard Munch, at US$124 million, and by the record-holder, *Portrait of Adele Bloch-Bauer I*, by Gustav Klimt. That's worth around US$154 million.

LOST LILIES

In 1958, workmen installing air conditioning on the second floor accidentally started a fire. Most of the paintings were moved to safety, but the huge *Water Lilies* painting by Monet had to be left behind because it was so big. It was damaged beyond repair, and art lovers sent letters of sympathy to the museum for the loss.

I'M THE ART

In 2010, performance artist Marina Abramovic sat silently in MoMA for 750 hours. Her performance art piece was called *The Artist Is Present*, and visitors could join in by sitting in front of her. People stood in line for hours for the chance to stare back at her!

BABY, THAT'S GOOD!
WHITNEY MUSEUM OF AMERICAN ART

The Whitney is the US's premier gallery of modern American art, with over 21,000 works by 3,000 US artists. It may be full of treasures, but the museum is eager for everyone to join the fun. On Saturdays, families get time to sketch pictures together, and even babies get in on the action. They have "stroller tours," when the museum closes to the rest of the public, allowing the tots to cry as much as they like, and their parents to admire the art!

WHITNEY MUSEUM OF AMERICAN ART

WORLD TRADE CENTER

SHINING TRIBUTE
WORLD TRADE CENTER

As dusk falls on September 11 each year, two powerful beams of blue light reach 4 miles (6.5 km) into the sky to mark the anniversary of the 2001 attack on the World Trade Center. The *Tribute in Light* art installation is made up of 88 powerful bulbs arranged in two 48-foot (14.6 m) squares that echo the shape of the Twin Towers. On a clear night, they can be seen over 60 miles (97 km) away.

THE GENERATORS THAT POWER THE *TRIBUTE IN LIGHT* ARE FUELED BY BIODIESEL MADE FROM USED COOKING OIL COLLECTED FROM LOCAL RESTAURANTS.

PLAYING THE BUILDING
BATTERY MARITIME BUILDING

In 2008, musician David Byrne transformed the Battery Maritime Building into a giant musical instrument, so visitors could play the building as a sound sculpture! Hoses attached to an old pump organ blew air into the pipes, making them hoot and whistle. Hammers and motors clanged against columns. The echoing sound produced was really quite creepy.

BATTERY MARITIME BUILDING

DAG HAMMARSKJÖLD PLAZA

ART ADDED HERE
DAG HAMMARSKJÖLD PLAZA

There's outdoor art all over New York, and it changes from year to year. In 2015, for instance, you could see a giant 9-foot (2.7 m) see-through Hello Kitty in the plaza. Japanese artist Sebastian Masuda wanted local people to get involved and add objects to his *Time After Time Capsule*, gradually filling it. The piece will be on display at the 2020 Tokyo Olympics, along with sculptures filled in other cities.

search: OUTDOOR ART
ART FOR EVERYONE!

New York's Parks Department presents art exhibitions in the city's parks, using them as outdoor galleries so the art is available to everyone who goes there. An amazing range of artwork styles and materials is used, from huge steel structures to biodegradable artworks that decay over time!

THE GIANT SNAIL
GUGGENHEIM MUSEUM

The Guggenheim has been compared to a multistory car park, a snail, and an upside-down beehive. The spiral gallery wraps around the building from the ground to the ceiling and, at first, artists worried that its curved walls and sloping floors would make it impossible to hang their paintings straight. When the exterior of the building was restored in 2007, leftover fragments were made into jewelry.

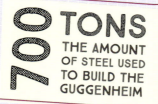

700 TONS THE AMOUNT OF STEEL USED TO BUILD THE GUGGENHEIM

7,000 CUBIC FEET (198 CUBIC METERS) THE AMOUNT OF POURED CONCRETE USED IN THE BUILDING

GUGGENHEIM MUSEUM

MUSEUM OF THE CITY OF NEW YORK

MINI-MASTERPIECE
MUSEUM OF THE CITY OF NEW YORK

The Stettheimer Dollhouse was given to the Museum of the City of New York in 1945. Artist Carrie Walter Stettheimer took 25 years to make it, crafting wallpaper, teeny pots and pans, crystal-trimmed candelabra, and Limoges vases. But what makes it really special are the tiny paintings and sculptures within its walls. Some of Carrie's friends were famous artists, and made minuscule works of art for it.

CONCRETE CANVAS
GRAFFITI HALL OF FAME

This outdoor gallery was founded in an East Harlem schoolyard by New York graffiti artist Ray Rodríguez (aka Sting Ray) back in 1980. It's since become a who's who of street artists. Each year a talented crew gets together to repaint the walls. The gallery is free to visit whenever the school is closed.

HERE TODAY, GONE TOMORROW
LOCATIONS AROUND THE CITY

World-famous graffiti artist Banksy came to New York in 2013 and created art all over the city for a month. Reportedly, the NY police were on his tail, but they never caught him and he managed to leave behind all kinds of street art, including a spray-painting robot, a man with a bunch of flowers, and some figures who appeared to be washing graffiti off a wall.

THERE ARE LOTS OF THEORIES ABOUT WHO BANKSY IS, BUT HIS IDENTITY IS A WELL-KEPT SECRET. IT IS THOUGHT HE WAS BORN IN BRISTOL, UK, AROUND 1974.

85

STREET SCULPTURE

Street sculpture is big in New York, with over 300 examples to be admired around town. Here's where you can discover some of the stories behind the city's most famous sculpture stars.

FABULOUS FOUR
GROUP OF FOUR TREES, CHASE MANHATTAN PLAZA

There's a magical forest right in the heart of New York's busy financial district. It's Jean Dubuffet's black and white tree sculpture in front of the Chase Manhattan Building. The trees look like a 3D coloring book – a drawing come to life. It's been seen as a symbol of nature and of creativity, too. After all, anything is possible in a place where magical trees appear!

CHASE MANHATTAN PLAZA

THE BIG BULL
CHARGING BULL, BOWLING GREEN PARK

In 1989, this fierce-looking bull surprised everyone by appearing in front of the New York Stock Exchange. The artist, Arturo Di Modica, made it to symbolize US financial optimism and strength, and gave it as a Christmas present to the city. The police took it away, but the public demanded it back, and now it has found a home in a place where tourists can gather. In fact, the bull is so popular its nose has become shiny where people have rubbed it for good luck.

BOWLING GREEN PARK

11 FT. (3.5 M) TALL
16 FT. (4.9 M) LONG
WEIGHT 7,100 LB. (3,200 KG)

BEAUTIFUL BALLOON

BALLOON FLOWER (RED), 7 WORLD TRADE CENTER

New York superstar artist Jeff Koons created this gorgeous sculpture *Balloon Flower (Red)*, and installed it in a fountain. The sculpture is made of stainless steel, but it's so shiny that it looks like a stretchy twisted balloon. A similar balloon sculpture by Koons sold for over US$58.4 million, but New Yorkers cherish this one because its bright, cheerful color brightens up the dark days of winter.

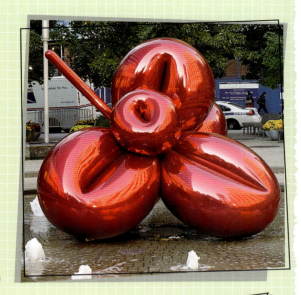

WORLD TRADE CENTER

ASTOR PLACE

COOL CUBE

ALAMO, ASTOR PLACE

This giant black steel cube, titled *Alamo*, has 8-foot (2.4 m) square sides and an unusual feature. It's possible to slowly turn it around on its axis. In the past it's been decorated to look like a Rubik's Cube and been wrapped in knitting as a protest. It's even had a fake documentary made about it, claiming someone was living inside it.

A QUESTION OF TIME
THE METRONOME, UNION SQUARE

This amazing art installation is designed to make people think about time. It's a crazy clock, with a digital display of 15 numbers and a hole that puffs out steam at noon and midnight. The big bronze hand at the top was cast from the equestrian statue of George Washington in the park below and enlarged. The rings in the wall are made to look like the ripples in a pool of water. Each one is made of carefully crafted panels of brick, each weighing up to 29 tons.

LUNCHTIME!

HOW TO READ THE CLOCK
➔ Reading from the left-hand side, the digits display the **hours**, **minutes**, and **seconds** since midnight.
➔ From the right, going backwards, the digits tell the number of **hours**, **minutes**, and **seconds** away from midnight.
➔ The fast-moving middle digits count **fifths of a second**.

UNION SQUARE

PORT AUTHORITY BUS TERMINAL

MOVING MAGIC
42ND STREET BALLROOM, PORT AUTHORITY BUS TERMINAL

Passengers waiting for their buses can spend time watching 16 pool balls trundling around tubes and tracks in this giant box, built by sculptor George Rhoads. It's a "kinetic sculpture," which means it moves. Onlookers say it's soothing to watch, so it sounds like perfect panic protection amid the hustle and bustle of a busy bus station. You can try its soothing effect at home by finding it online.

GIRAFFES FOR PEACE
PEACE FOUNTAIN, AMSTERDAM AVE.

Here's a fountain that's truly unlike any other. It includes a giant crab, a sun and moon, a DNA spiral, a lion and a lamb, a giant angel who has killed the Devil... oh, and nine giraffes! Each feature has a symbolic meaning related to the triumph of good over evil in the world. Why giraffes? Because they are very peaceful animals, according to sculptor Greg Wyatt.

search: UNISPHERE

VITAL STATS
140 ft. (43 m) high, 120 ft. (37 m) in diameter, and 900,000 lb. (408,233 kg) in weight, including the base

DESIGN
The sphere is an open grid design, with curved sheets of stainless steel for the landmasses. The capital cities of the larger nations are indicated by lights.

AMSTERDAM AVE.

FLUSHING MEADOWS

STEEL IN SPACE
UNISPHERE, FLUSHING MEADOWS–CORONA PARK

Not only is the *Unisphere* the biggest globe structure in the world, it's featured in loads of movies, rock videos, and even computer games. This stainless steel see-through model of Earth was built in the 1960s to represent the achievements of mankind in the space age. The pool beneath it and fountains around it are designed to make it appear as if it's floating in space.

SHOP 'TIL YOU DROP

New York and shopping go together like burgers and fries. You'll find almost everything on your wish list in this shopaholic's paradise... and since no trip to New York is complete without a visit to Macy's, let's start there!

HISTORIC SHOPPING

MACY'S, HERALD SQUARE

Macy's was founded in 1843 and its flagship store opened in Herald Square in 1902. At the time, this was so far from other stores that the shop had to provide a wagon to ferry customers uptown. Now Macy's takes up a whole block in what has become one of the city's busiest shopping districts. It was one of the first places in the US to have an escalator, and some of the old wooden escalators are still in use today.

HERALD SQUARE

STAR SAILOR

Macy's star logo is said to be based on a tattoo of the store's founder, Rowland Macy. He had the tattoo done as a teenager while he was working as a seaman on a whaling ship.

TITANIC TRAGEDY

Brothers Isidor and Nathan Straus bought the store from the Macy family in 1895. Isidor and his wife were on the *Titanic* when it sank in 1912, and they both drowned after giving up their lifeboat seats. Macy's employees helped fund a memorial plaque for their popular boss and his wife. It says "Their lives were beautiful and their deaths glorious" and can be seen in Macy's memorial entrance on 34th Street.

EYE-POPPING PARADE

Every year Macy's hosts a spectacular three-hour Thanksgiving Day Parade, watched by millions on TV across the US. Santa Claus always makes the trip to NY for the parade, and at the end he is welcomed into Herald Square. The parade is famous for its giant helium-filled balloons, some so big they need up to 90 balloon handlers!

3.8 MILLION STREETSIDE SPECTATORS
(ESTIMATED NUMBER EACH YEAR)

MACY'S IN THE MOVIES

Macy's starred in the 1947 film *Miracle on 34th Street*, which shows the actual 1946 Macy's Thanksgiving Day Parade. The crowd didn't know that actor Edmund Gwenn was playing Santa in the parade, as he did in the film. The 1966 comedy *You're a Big Boy Now* includes a chase through the store. The film crew used hidden cameras, but didn't tell anyone so they could capture the genuine reactions of staff and shoppers to the mayhem.

CHELSEA FLEA MARKET

search: STRAND BOOK STORE

2.5 MILLION
Approx. number of books in the store.

US$45,000
Price of the most expensive rare book in the store.

STRAND BOOK STORE

TREASURE HUNT
CHELSEA FLEA MARKET

New Yorkers with an eye for a bargain head out to the city's flea markets, such as the Chelsea Flea Market. There they can rummage through the stalls piled high with vintage collectibles, including clothing, jewelry, and antique oddities. Haggling and people-watching are all part of the fun, along with the thought that something rare and valuable might be waiting for you...

A BOOK-LOVER'S DREAM
STRAND BOOK STORE

If you've ever wondered what 2.5 million books look like, take a trip to the Strand Book Store. Here, new, used, and rare books stretch across approximately 18 miles (29 km) of shelves on three floors. Imagine having to tidy those up. Not surprisingly, the beloved bookshop has featured in movies, songs, and, yes... books!

LOLLIPOP LAND
ECONOMY CANDY

WHEN ECONOMY CANDY OPENED IN 1937, IT WAS A SHOE AND HAT REPAIR SHOP, TOO.

Economy Candy is the oldest candy store in New York City, and it's packed from floor to ceiling with lollipops, salt water taffy, chocolate bars, and a whole zoo of gummy treats. There are free goodies for kids in costume at Halloween, and those looking for a blast from the past come here to find vintage comics, trading cards, gumball machines, and board games, alongside the classic sweet treats.

ECONOMY CANDY

BROOKLYN SUPERHERO SUPPLY CO.

SUPERHERO SHOP
BROOKLYN SUPERHERO SUPPLY CO.

When superheroes run out of X-ray vision power or need to try out a cape in a cape-testing wind tunnel, they head for the Brooklyn Superhero Supply Co. Here they can buy superpowers, such as magnetism, or stock up on superhero basics like antimatter. The shop has an alter ego, too – just like Superman or Batman. A hidden door leads to the headquarters of 826NYC, the superhero base of storytellers and workshop leaders who work with thousands of NY schoolchildren to encourage their writing skills.

JACKSON HEIGHTS

FAIRYTALE SALE
SOTHEBY'S AUCTION HOUSE

Sotheby's is most famous for its record-breaking art sales, but in 2007 it sold a copy of *The Tales of Beedle the Bard*, handwritten and illustrated by J. K. Rowling, for an incredible US$3,835,980! The book of wizarding fairy tales was mentioned in the Harry Potter series and only seven handmade copies exist.

SOTHEBY'S AUCTION HOUSE

IN 2012, SOTHEBY'S NEW YORK SOLD EDVARD MUNCH'S PAINTING *THE SCREAM* FOR US$119,922,500.

INDIA COMES TO NY
JACKSON HEIGHTS

On 74th Street there's a slice of India along the "Little India" road. The delicious smell of Indian food wafts from nearby restaurants, the latest Bollywood music plays, and the strip is lined with shops selling Indian clothes and jewelry. Rainbow-colored lengths of sari fabric fill the windows and line the shop walls. It's said there are over 50 ways to wear a sari, and here's where to find the experts.

WHERE IT'S RARE
BRIGANDI COIN COMPANY

Brigandi's is THE store for seekers of rare coins and memorabilia. The rarest coins on sale there are worth many thousands of dollars, so remember to never throw away an old coin without checking its value first! Brigandi's also specializes in sports memorabilia, such as baseball bats and shirts signed by top players. If you ever find a ball, bat, or card signed by New York Yankee legend Babe Ruth, Brigandi's will want to hear from you. These are among the most sought-after sporting treasures.

FAIRWAY MARKET, HARLEM

NO-SHIVER SHOPPING
FAIRWAY MARKET, HARLEM

When Nathan Glickberg started a little fruit and vegetable stand in 1933, he could never have imagined that it would become a grocery chain with 14 million customers a year. Fairway's flagship Harlem store has a huge 10,000-square-foot (929 sq m) cold room, plus a stack of warm jackets to lend to chilly cold-room customers. The owners haven't forgotten the store's humble beginnings and regularly donate goods to local shelters and food banks.

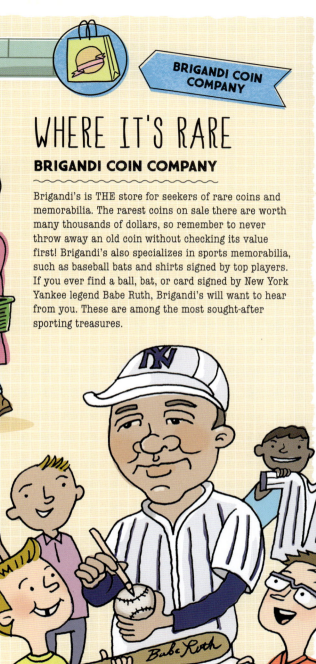

MOVIE MAGIC

For movie fans, walking around New York sometimes feels like being on a giant movie set. That's because it's starred as a backdrop for countless movies. Here are just a few of its biggest screen triumphs. Lights! Camera! Action!

WHO YOU GONNA CALL?
TRIBECA FIREHOUSE, NORTH MOORE STREET

TRIBECA FIREHOUSE, NORTH MOORE ST.

The 1984 hit *Ghostbusters* was shot all over New York, but this fire station was used as the headquarters of the silly spook hunters. There is now an emblem on the sidewalk out front to commemorate its movie identity. Inside it's a working fire station, not a ghostly hangout. The inside of the Ghostbuster base was actually shot in Los Angeles.

THE BIG APE BUILDING
EMPIRE STATE BUILDING

The Empire State became one of the most famous movie sets of all time when King Kong climbed up it in 1933. In reality, the movie scene was filmed on a set in Hollywood. The movie was incredibly innovative and used all sorts of tricks to create the effects it needed. The King Kong shown climbing up the building was a mini-model covered in rabbit fur!

START

EMPIRE STATE BUILDING

FOR THE 50TH ANNIVERSARY OF KING KONG, A GIANT INFLATABLE GORILLA WAS PUT ON TOP OF THE EMPIRE STATE BUILDING, BUT A TEAR AT THE SHOULDER MADE IT DEFLATE. OOPS!

AMERICAN MUSEUM OF NATURAL HISTORY

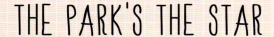

CENTRAL PARK

THE PARK'S THE STAR
CENTRAL PARK

One of the first movies ever made in the US, *Romeo and Juliet* was filmed in Central Park over a century ago, in 1908. Since then, hundreds of movies have been shot here, with visits from *Spider-Man*, *Men in Black*, *Godzilla*, *The Smurfs*, and *Stuart Little*, among many others. The animals in the 2005 movie *Madagascar* lived here, at the Central Park Zoo, before they escaped.

OVERNIGHT SENSATION
AMERICAN MUSEUM OF NATURAL HISTORY

The American Museum of Natural History is the star location for *Night at the Museum*, which came out in 2006. The movie wasn't really filmed in the museum, but the set designers studied the building closely to re-create it in a studio. Some of the movie characters were made up, but the stuffed animals and the Easter Island stone head all live at the museum for real.

COLUMBIA UNIVERSITY

THE CORE OF THE ROAR
COLUMBIA UNIVERSITY

You'll see a roaring lion at the beginning of films made by movie company MGM. That's Leo the Lion, the company mascot. He's said to be named after Columbia University's athletics team – "the Lions." The ad man who came up with the logo idea had attended the university, and used the team name as his starting point. Incidentally, the *Ghostbusters* characters were thrown out of Columbia University and came up with their crazy ghostbusting idea on the Low Library steps outside.

QUEENSBORO BRIDGE

SPIDER-MAN'S CITY
QUEENSBORO BRIDGE AND ROOSEVELT ISLAND TRAM

Marvel Comics' famous superhero Spider-Man is a New York boy. His alter ego, Peter Parker, was born in Queens and then went to live with his aunt and uncle in Forest Hills. When the movie *Spider-Man* was released in 2002, it featured a thrilling scene in which Spider-Man's enemy, the Goblin, held people hostage on a Roosevelt Island tram, next to the Queensboro Bridge.

search: ROOSEVELT ISLAND TRAM

TEMPORARY TRAM
Built in 1976, the tramway was a temporary means of transporting people to and from Manhattan, until the subway station was completed. But when the subway finally opened, the tram had become too popular to close down.

HOME OF THE MUPPETS

MUSEUM OF THE MOVING IMAGE

This museum is all about everything movie-related. Visitors can go behind the scenes, see costumes, and even try out special effects for themselves. It's also the home of the Muppets, the puppet stars of TV and movies created by puppet-making genius Jim Henson. The original puppets of Kermit, Miss Piggy, Elmo, and friends all live here!

MUSEUM OF THE MOVING IMAGE

FLUSHING MEADOWS–CORONA PARK

ALIEN SAUCER PARK

NEW YORK PAVILION, FLUSHING MEADOWS–CORONA PARK

This mysterious-looking site has an alien secret. Back in the 1960s, three towers with observation decks on top gave visitors an "Astro-View" of the park, and they still stand in a circle of pillars called "The Tent of Tomorrow." In 1997, Will Smith and Tommy Lee Jones arrived here in the movie *Men in Black*. They discovered the observation decks were alien spaceships about to take off! There's a big debate as to whether the towers should be restored or pulled down. One day those alien spaceships may really disappear...

INDEX

Alamo 87
American Indians 16
American Museum of Natural History ......
   32-3, 48, 97
animals 24, 25, 30-35
Apollo Theater 55
art 28, 38, 48, 69, 80-89
Arthur Ashe Stadium 73
Atlantic Avenue subway 19

bagels 40
ballet 53
Balloon Flower (Red) 87
Balto (dog sculpture) 25
Banksy 85
baseball 42, 70, 74-5
basketball 72
Battery Maritime Building 83
bells 6, 79
bike rental 59
Blessing of the Animals 31
"Bloody Angle" 17
Bowling Green Park 86
Brigandi Coin Company 95
Broadway 50-51, 71
Bronx Zoo 30
Brooklyn 35, 40, 73
Brooklyn Botanic Garden 20
Brooklyn Bridge 62
Brooklyn Bridge Park 77

Brooklyn Superhero Supply Co. 93
buried treasure 19, 49, 60
Burr, Aaron 67, 68
buses 58
buskers 37

Canyon of Heroes 71
Carnegie Hall 76
carousel 77
Cathedral of St. John the Divine 31
cattle tunnel 36
caves 16
cemeteries 35, 69
Central Park 24-5, 31, 45, 54,
   56, 60, 70, 77, 97
Charging Bull 86
cheesecake 43
Chelsea Flea Market 92
Chinatown 17, 41
Chinese Scholar's Garden 21
chocolate 43
Chrysler Building 12
churches 31, 79
Citi Bike Station 59
city grid system 6
City Hall Old Station 36
City Reliquary 46
Columbia University 98
Columbus Circle 9
Coney Island 44, 70

coywolves 30

Dag Hammarskjöld Plaza 83
dance marathons 52
Delacorte Clock 77
delicatessens 42, 43
dinosaurs 32-3
Drummer's Grove 78

Economy Candy 93
Empire State Building 12, 96, 97
Enterprise space shuttle 61

Fairway Market 95
farm, city 20, 25
Federal Reserve Bank 18
ferries 63
Flag 81
Flatiron Building 13
Floyd Bennett Field 19
Flushing Meadows–Corona Park 89, 99
food 40-45
food-vending carts 45
Ford Foundation Greenhouse 17
Fresh Kills Landfill 28

Gardener's Island 49
Ghostbusters 96, 98
ghosts and legends 19, 23, 49, 52, 66-9
gold bars 18

Governors Island 34
Gowanus Canal 62
graffiti 85
Gramercy Park 22
Grand Central Terminal 16, 27, 58, 68, 72
Greenacre Park 23
Greenwich Village 7
Green-Wood Cemetery 35
Group of Four Trees 86
Guggenheim Museum 84

Halloween 69
Hangman's Elm 66
Harlem 26, 55, 78, 95
Hell's Gate 60
High Line 23
hip-hop 76
horse-drawn carriages 56
hot dogs 44–5
Hudson River 60

ice cream 41
ice hockey 72
Intrepid Sea, Air & Space Museum 61

jazz 78
jewels 47, 48
Juilliard 53
Junior's Deli 43

Katz's Deli 42
Kidd, Captain 49
Kool Herc's House 76

libraries 46, 47
Life Underground 38
Li-Lac Chocolate Factory 43
Lincoln Center 53
Little India 94
Liz Christy Community Garden 21
Long Island 49, 57
lost and found 27

Macy's 90–91
Madison Square Garden 72
Madonna and Child 48
Manhattan 6, 8, 18, 21, 23, 24–5, 49, 73
Marathon 70
Marionette Theatre 54
Merchant's House Museum 66
Metronome 88
Metropolitan Museum of Art 38, 48
Metropolitan Opera House 79
Morgan Library 46
Morris-Jumel Mansion 67, 68
movies 61, 66, 96–9
MTV Studios 52
Museum of Modern Art (MoMA) 80–81

Museum of the City of New York 84
Museum of the Moving Image 99
museums 10, 15, 16, 20, 26, 32–3, 38, 39, 46, 48–9, 61, 66, 80–81, 82, 84, 97, 99
music 38, 53, 76–9, 83

narrowest house 7
National Museum of the American Indian 16
National September 11 Memorial 15
Newton Creek 29
New Victory Theater 52
New Year 50
New York Aquarium 35
New York Botanical Garden 69
New York Earth Room 22
New York Harbor 60–63
New York Public Library 47
New York Yankees 70, 74–5
Nikola Tesla Corner 7
9/11 Museum 15

One World Trade Center 14–15
opera 79

Paley Park 23
parakeets 35
parks and gardens 17, 20–25, 28, 30, 31, 54, 56, 66, 69, 77, 83, 99

101

INDEX

pastrami 42
Peace Fountain 89
pedestrian walkways 8
pedicabs 59
Pelham Bay Park 22
Phantom of the Opera (The) ... 51
pickles 41
pizzas 40, 41
Plaza Hotel 57
pneumatic trash tubes 26
Port Authority Bus Terminal ... 58, 88
Prospect Park 78
puppet theater 54

Queens County Farm Museum ... 20
Queens Museum of Art 10
Queensboro Bridge 98

Radio City Music Hall 34
rats 29
Red Hook Ball Fields 42
Robbins Reef Light 63
Rockefeller Center 11, 34
roller derby 73
Roosevelt, F. D. 68
Roosevelt Island 26, 98

Sailors' Snug Harbor 23, 63
St. Patrick's Cathedral 79
sewage system 29

Shakespeare, William 54
ships 60, 61
shopping 90–95
skyscrapers 10–15
SLAM 71
soccer 71
Sotheby's Auction House 94
South Street Seaport 61
sports 70–75
Star of India 48
Staten Island 28, 63, 70
Statue of Liberty 64–5, 71
steam tunnels 18
Stettheimer Dollhouse 84
stickball 9
Stock Exchange 6
Strand Book Store 92
subway 19, 36–9
Swedish Cottage 54

talent contests 55
taxis 56, 57
tennis 73
Thanksgiving Parade 91
theaters 50–55
ticker-tape parades 71
Tiffany's 47
Times Square 50
Tony Awards 51
Transit Museum 39

transportation 36–9, 56–9, 63
trash 26–9
Trash Museum 26
treasures 46–9
Tribeca Firehouse 96
Tribute in Light 82
Turtle Pond 31
Twain, Mark 67, 69

UN (United Nations) headquarters ... 8
underground New York 36–9
Union Square Station 37
Unisphere 89

Van Cortlandt Park 30

Wall Street 6
Washington Square Park 66
Whispering Gallery 16
Whitney Museum of American Art ... 82
Winnie-the-Pooh 47
Woodlawn Cemetery 69
Woolworth Building 13
World Trade Center 14, 82

Yankee Stadium 74–5
yellow cabs 56, 57

zoos 30, 77